D1609225

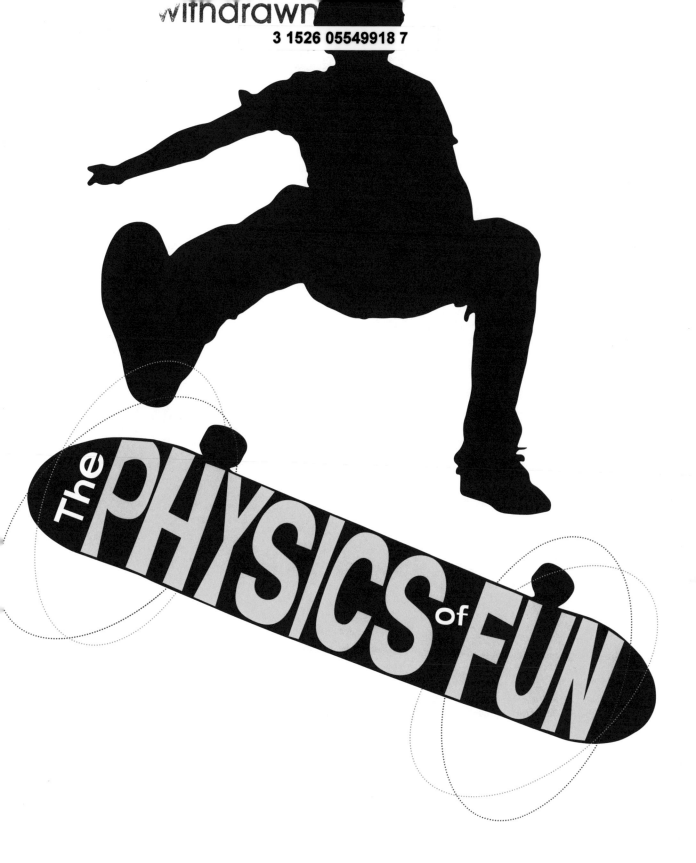

The PHYSICS of FUN

Carla Mooney

Illustrated by Alexis Cornell

Nomad Press

A division of Nomad Communications

10 9 8 7 6 5 4 3 2 1

This book was manufactured by Versa Press,
East Peoria, Illinois, United States
October 2021, Job #J21-05590

ISBN Softcover: 978-1-64741-034-6
ISBN Hardcover: 978-1-64741-031-5

Educational Consultant, Marla Conn

Questions regarding the ordering of this book should be addressed to
Nomad Press
PO Box 1036, Norwich, VT 05055
www.nomadpress.net

Printed in the United States.

More physics titles from Nomad Press

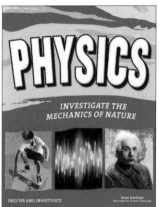

Check out more titles at www.nomadpress.net

You can use a smartphone or tablet app to scan the QR codes and explore more! Cover up neighboring QR codes to make sure you're scanning the right one. You can find a list of URLs on the Resources page.

If the QR code doesn't work, try searching the internet with the Keyword Prompts to find other helpful sources.

Interested in primary sources? **Look for this icon.**

🔍 physics of fun

Contents

TIMELINE

Third Century BCE: Greek astronomer Aristarchus suggests that the sun, not the earth, is the center of the solar system.

1512: Polish astronomer Nicholas Copernicus presents his heliocentric theory, which places the sun at the center of the solar system. He proposes that the earth travels around the sun once a year and rotates daily on its axis.

1609: Italian mathematician and physicist Galileo Galilei builds a powerful telescope that is able to see the moons orbiting Jupiter and sunspots on the sun.

1613: Galileo first describes the principle of inertia.

1668: English mathematician John Wallis presents the law of conservation of momentum.

1675: English physicist Sir Isaac Newton argues that light is composed of particles.

1687: Newton publishes his laws of motion and law of universal gravitation.

1752: American philosopher and scientist Benjamin Franklin performs his famous kite and key experiment, which demonstrates that lightning is actually a form of electricity.

1800: Italian physicist Alessandro Volta invents the electric battery, which provides the first source of continuous current.

1801: English scientist Thomas Young demonstrates the interference of light and concludes that light is made of waves.

1826: German physicist and mathematician George Ohm presents the law of electrical resistance.

1888: German physicist Heinrich Hertz proves the existence of electromagnetic waves.

1895: German mechanical engineer and physicist Wilhelm Conrad Rontgen discovers X-rays.

1897: British physicist Joseph John Thomson discovers the electron, the first subatomic particle.

1900: German physicist Max Planck develops his quantum theory of energy.

1905: German physicist Albert Einstein publishes his theory of relativity and ideas about light and the universe.

1915: Einstein includes a description of gravity in his theory of relativity.

1934: George Nissen and Larry Griswold build the first modern trampoline at the University of Iowa.

Early 1950s: Surfers in California create the first skateboards using wooden boards and rollerskate wheels.

1958: American physicist Charles Townes invents the laser.

1981: The first national snowboarding competition is held at Ski Cooper in Leadville, Colorado.

1995: Researchers from ETH Zurich in Switzerland and the University of Tokyo in Japan demonstrate quantum teleportation, a technique for transferring quantum information from one location to a receiver in another location.

1997: An international team of scientists finds evidence of an anti-gravity force that is causing the universe to expand at an accelerating rate.

1998: Snowboarding makes its Olympic debut in Nagano, Japan.

2012: Scientists at CERN, a particle physics lab near Geneva, Switzerland, make the first discovery of a Higgs boson particle.

2016: Scientists prove the existence of gravitational waves, which are ripples in space-time that come from objects moving throughout the universe.

Introduction

The World Runs on Science

Why is physics a fundamental science?

Physics is part of everything!
Biology, chemistry, meteorology, astronomy—every other science relies on the basics of physics.

What do you do for fun? Maybe you like to ride a skateboard, jump on a trampoline, or play the latest video games. Have you ever wondered how you can stay on top of the skateboard without falling off? Or why you can jump three times as high from a trampoline as from the ground? Or how video games are powered?

All of these questions can be explained by physics!

Many people do not think "fun" and "physics" go together. When they think of physics, they imagine complicated equations and laboratory experiments. In reality, physics doesn't just happen in a lab. Physics is all around us. Every time you move, you are using physics.

Do you play basketball? You're using physics every time you step on the court to shoot a free throw. Do you like hockey? Physics is part of every shot and save on the ice.

In fact, physics is part of everything you do, from walking the dog to sledding down a hill to playing the guitar. Learning physics can help us understand the world around us and how it works.

WHAT IS PHYSICS?

Physics is the study of matter and its motion and energy. Matter is anything that has mass and takes up space. Matter is all around you—including your own body! This book is made of matter. Your skateboard is made of matter. The air you breathe, the water you drink, and the food you eat are made of matter.

Everything on Earth, in the solar system, and in the universe is made of matter.

Before scientists better understood physics, most people assumed that nature was controlled by a supernatural or religious source.

•••••••••••••••••••••••••••••••••••

Scientists who study physics, called physicists, seek to understand how matter and the natural universe work. In fact, the word *physics* comes from a Greek word that means "nature." Physicists analyze and explain the world's natural phenomena, which are things that are observed or perceived. They perform and repeat experiments to study scientific laws, which are statements that describe how the natural world works.

These scientific laws, such as the laws of gravity and Newton's laws of motion, have been tested so much that scientists accept them as scientific truths. Physicists use these scientific laws to predict how other things will behave.

Physics is a physical science. It is also known as the fundamental science, because it forms a basis for all other sciences, including chemistry, biology, and astronomy.

Without physics, the chemists, biologists, and astronomers would not be able to do their work!

Physics has helped us better understand and predict natural phenomena in the world around us. Because of physics, we can explain why the sky is blue and a rose is red. We understand weather and know how to predict it, to a certain extent. We have learned how to predict and prepare for natural disasters such as earthquakes, hurricanes, and tornadoes.

We can use our knowledge about what happens in a collision to design safety equipment to reduce damage. We can even predict what happens if you shoot a free throw, hit a baseball, or skate across a frozen pond. All because of physics!

Energy is the ability to do work, such as pushing an object up a hill or plucking a guitar string.

AN ANCIENT AND MODERN SCIENCE

People have been studying physics for centuries. The ancient Greeks are considered to be the founders of early physics. Great thinkers such as Socrates (circa 470–399 BCE), Plato (circa 428–348 BCE), and Aristotle (384–322 BCE) pushed to better understand the natural world around them. They tried to explain what matter is made of and how it moves.

They observed the world and developed explanations for what they observed.

Quantum physics is the study of the microscopic world and its particles. This branch of physics has led to the development of the laser, the internet, modern electronics, and more.

Many years later, during the 1500s and 1600s, scientists such as Nicolaus Copernicus (1473–1543), Galileo Galilei (1564–1642), and Sir Isaac Newton (1643–1727) devoted their lives to the study of physics. They made lots of important discoveries about the natural world, many of which formed the foundation of modern physics today.

Copernicus demonstrated that the earth orbits the sun. Galileo described many fundamental physics concepts and tested his ideas about motion.

Galileo and his telescope. Some of his astronomical discoveries are shown in the sky.

Primary sources come from people who were eyewitnesses to events. They might write about the event, take videos, post messages to social media, or record the sound of an event. For example, the photographs in this book are primary sources, taken at the time of the event. Paintings of events are usually not primary sources, since they were often painted long after the event took place. They are secondary sources. Why do you think primary sources are important?

Galileo also greatly improved the design of the telescope, which allowed scientists to make many new astronomical discoveries. Galileo lived during a period known as the Scientific Revolution, which lasted from about 1550 to 1700, when a series of discoveries in mathematics, physics, astronomy, biology, and chemistry caused whole societies to think differently about the nature of the universe. Other scientists during the Scientific Revolution performed experiments to prove Galileo's ideas.

Sir Isaac Newton developed his own three laws of motion and the law of universal gravitation. According to Newton's law of gravity, every object with mass in the universe is attracted to every other object with mass.

This attraction between objects is called gravity. How strong or weak that pull of gravity is depends on the mass of the objects and how close they are to each other.

After Newton, other scientists made discoveries about light, heat, radiation, electromagnetics, and other forces. During the nineteenth and twentieth centuries, some scientists studied the physics of very tiny particles of matter and energy, down to the subatomic level.

> **FLIP FACT**
>
> Nuclear physics is the study of the atom's center, the nucleus. This branch of physics has led to important discoveries in medicine, energy, and the environment.

The study of physics is the science of how matter and energy interact and work together, no matter how large or small the size of an object.

Without physics, many of today's technologies would not be possible. The study of physics made it possible to develop lasers, televisions, radios, computers, smartphones, and more. Today, scientists are using physics to improve our daily lives further as they work on new technologies, ideas, and products. Physicists strive to develop and improve products and manufacturing processes in industries such as healthcare, energy, transportation, defense, manufacturing, and telecommunications.

Physicists are also working with energy companies to develop new and efficient energy systems to harness Earth's sustainable energy. Some physicists focus on studying the earth and weather, while others are making discoveries in space and astronomy.

What does all this have to do with fun? Well, everything around you is made of matter. Physics explains what happens when matter is in motion. Every time you move, jump, or blow into a trumpet, you are using physics!

The activities in this book will introduce you to the concepts that are used to explain the energy and motion of matter. We'll take a look at skateboarding, snowboarding, trampolining, playing an instrument, and more to discover how the laws of physics make it possible to do all of these fun activities.

Ready? Let's go!

SCIENTIFIC METHOD

The scientific method is the process scientists use to ask questions and find answers. Keep a science journal to record your methods and observations during all the activities in this book. You can use a scientific method worksheet to keep your ideas and observations organized.

Question: What are we trying to find out? What problem are we trying to solve?

Research: What is already known about this topic?

Hypothesis: What do we think the answer will be?

Equipment: What supplies are we using?

Method: What procedure are we following?

Results: What happened and why?

KEY QUESTIONS

- **How has physics improved your life?**
- **Why does the study of physics affect so many other fields of science?**

TEXT TO WORLD

Think of three things you do for fun that involve physics. How do you know?

Inquire & Investigate

VOCAB LAB 📖

Write down what you think each word means. What root words can you find to help you? What does the context of the word tell you?

energy, **friction**, **fundamental science**, **gravity**, **matter**, and **physics**.

Compare your definitions with those of your friends or classmates. Did you all come up with the same meanings? Turn to the text and glossary if you need help.

To investigate more, experiment with different objects sliding down the ramp. What happens? What conclusions can you make?

EXPLORE FRICTION ON A RAMP

One part of physics that affects everything you do is friction! Friction is a force that occurs when two surfaces rub against each other. Smoother surfaces generate less friction, while rough or bumpy surfaces generate more friction. Check it out!

- **Create a ramp with stacked books and plywood or cardboard.** Make sure there is empty space at the end of the ramp.

- **Starting with the smooth plywood or cardboard, release a toy car from the top of the ramp.** Measure how far the car travels from the top of the ramp to where it stops. Record the results in your science notebook. Repeat two more times, and, using the three distances, calculate the average distance traveled by adding up all of the distances and dividing that number by the number of runs you did.

- **Place something bumpy, such as sandpaper or a towel, on the ramp's surface.** Tape it down so it doesn't move. Repeat running the car down the ramp over the test surface three times and find the average distance.

- **Repeat this process for more test materials, such as carpet pieces or clothing.** Calculate the average distance traveled for each material.

- **Compare your results.** How did the car travel on each surface? On which surfaces did it travel farther? On which surfaces did it travel less? Based on your experiment, what did you learn about the friction of the different test surfaces?

Chapter 1

Forces of Skateboarding

IT'S MORE THAN JUST DOING SWEET FLIPS!

What kinds of forces are needed for skateboarding?

Skateboarders use lots of different types of forces—including gravity, spinning, and friction—to get the skateboard started and do their tricks!

Are you ready to spin, slide, and stick the trick on a skateboard? Maybe a simple ride down a hill is more your speed. No matter the style, skateboarding can be a lot of fun. And physics makes it possible! Every time you ride, flip, turn, and twist on a skateboard, the fundamentals of physics play a big part in making these impressive tricks succeed. Let's take a closer look at the physics behind skateboards and some common skateboarding moves.

FORCES AT WORK

Forces are at work in our daily lives all around us. Every time you open a door, type on a keyboard, or ride a skateboard, you use forces.

A force is a push or pull on an object when it interacts with another object.

Whenever two objects interact, forces act on each of them. Forces make objects move and stop. They can make moving objects speed up or slow down. Forces can also make an object stay still. Physics is the study of forces and how they work.

Sometimes, forces act when two objects physically touch each other. Other times, forces act when two objects interact even though they are physically separated. An example of this second type of force is gravity. When you jump into the air, you are no longer physically touching the ground, but the force of gravity still pulls you toward the ground. Similarly, the gravitational pull between the sun and the planets exists even though they are separated by extremely large distances.

Forces are measured in units called newtons (N). One newton is equal to the amount of force needed to make an object that is 1 kilogram in mass accelerate 1 meter per second faster every second. The equation for this is:

$$1 \text{ newton} = 1 \text{ kg} \times 1 \text{ m/s}^2$$

APPLIED FORCE, GRAVITY, AND FRICTION

For most everyday objects, the main forces that affect motion include applied forces, gravity, and friction. All of these forces act on skaters and their skateboards as they roll down the street or flip into the air during a trick.

FORCE AS A VECTOR

A force is a vector, which means that it has both a magnitude (size) and direction. This means when describing the force used to push a chair, you'd talk about both the size of the push and its direction. In a diagram, a force is often represented by an arrow. The arrow points in the direction the force is acting and its length shows the force's magnitude.

Applied force is a force that is applied to an object by a person or another object. For example, when you push or pull an object, you create an applied force on the object that affects its motion.

Gravity is another force that affects motion. Gravity is the force of attraction between two objects that have mass. Gravity can act accross a distance—the objects do not need to be touching. If you live on planet Earth—and who doesn't?!—you are familiar with Earth's gravity. This force pulls objects toward the planet's center and prevents you from floating into space. The force of gravity also explains why, when you drop something, it falls to the ground instead of moving sideways or upward. While skateboarding or performing tricks, the skater and skateboard are always pulled toward the ground by the force of gravity.

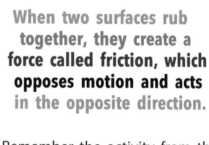

When two surfaces rub together, they create a force called friction, which opposes motion and acts in the opposite direction.

Remember the activity from the Introduction? What did you learn about friction? What creates it? First, you need to know that no surface is 100-percent smooth. Even something that looks smooth to the naked eye may be rough or bumpy when examined under a microscope. All of those bumps, no matter how microscopic, grab onto the bumps of any other object that they contact. When they do, the result is friction.

The amount of friction depends on the materials of the two surfaces rubbing together. A surface that is rougher—or bumpier—creates more friction than a smoother surface.

Have you ever tried to walk on ice with smooth-soled shoes? It's hard! Both surfaces are smooth and have fewer bumps to create friction. With less friction grabbing your shoes, you slip and slide! That's why people sprinkle sand on icy sidewalks and roads. The sand creates a rougher surface, which generates more friction when it comes into contact with shoes and tires. Pedestrians and cars are less likely to slide.

Friction helps a skater stand on top of a skateboard without slipping off. Sometimes, skateboarders even cover their board's deck with special pieces of sandpaper called grip tape. The rough surface of the grip tape increases the friction generated between the deck and the skateboarder's shoes, which reduces sliding and makes it easier to stay on the deck while riding.

FLIP FACT

Heavier objects that press against a surface with greater force create greater friction. That's why it's harder to push a heavy chair across the floor compared to a lighter chair.

COMBINING FORCES

In everyday life, objects often have more than one force acting on them at any given moment. Sometimes, forces act in opposite directions. Other times, they act in the same direction. The net force is the sum of all the forces acting on an object, with the forces acting in opposite directions cancelling each other out.

FOUR TYPES OF FRICTION

There are four types of friction: static, sliding, rolling, and fluid. Static friction acts on an object when it rests on a surface. In skateboarding, static friction occurs between the skater's shoes and the board. Sliding friction acts on objects as they slide over a surface. It is weaker than static friction. Rolling friction is even weaker, and acts on an object when it rolls over a surface. Fluid friction acts on objects moving through a fluid. When you push your hand through water, the resistance you feel against your hand is fluid friction. Air resistance is another example of fluid friction.

MASS VS. WEIGHT

Many people talk about mass and weight interchangeably, but they are different. An object's mass is the same no matter where it is. The object's weight, however, changes from place to place. Mass is a measurement of the amount of matter in an object and the amount of force needed to change its state of motion. In contrast, weight is the measurement of the downward force of gravity on an object. The force increases as the object's mass increases. Weight also changes based on the location of an object. For example, the force of gravity on the moon is weaker than on Earth, so astronauts weigh less there. Their mass, however, is the same.

Forces that act on an object can be balanced or unbalanced. Balanced forces occur when forces of equal strength act in opposite directions on the same object. In this case, the net force on the object is zero. The object does not move. Imagine you and your brother are standing on opposite sides of a door, pushing on it with the same amount of force. The forces are equal and opposite. They are also balanced, acting on the same object—the door. In this scenario, the forces cancel each other out and the door does not move.

What happens if your brother is feeling super strong and pushes harder on the door than you? The forces acting on the object—the door—become unbalanced and the door swings toward you. Unbalanced forces cause an object to change its speed, change its direction, or both. The net force acting on the object is the difference between the two forces causing the object to move in the direction of the larger force. The door responds to your brother's stronger force by moving in the direction he was pushing.

Imagine you and your brother are on the same side of the door, both of you pushing. What happens? That door doesn't stand a chance! When forces act on an object in the same direction, the net force is the sum of the two forces. It is greater than either of the individual forces.

LET'S GET STARTED

To see how applied force, gravity, and friction are involved in skateboarding, grab a skateboard from the garage and place it on flat pavement. No skateboard? No worries! You can find lots of videos demonstrating the physics of skateboarding online or simply use your imagination.

What happens when you carefully stand and balance on the skateboard's deck? Nothing. The board does not move across the flat pavement. You need an applied force to get things started!

To start the skateboard on flat pavement, you need to push off against the ground with one foot. That push generates an applied force that works on the board and acts in a specific direction. The harder the push, the greater the applied force that propels the board forward. At the same time, gravity pulls you and the board toward Earth.

Once you're rolling on a level surface, how do you stop? One easy way to stop is to let the board gradually slow down and roll to a stop.

Without any outside action, the board eventually stops because of friction **generated between the board's wheels and the ground. Friction pushes against** the wheels' motion and slows the board.

A rider can also stop their board by stepping on the back of it, so the board's deck scrapes the ground. This creates a lot of friction between the board and the ground, which works against the board's motion and slows it to a stop.

NEWTON'S LAWS OF MOTION

SIR ISAAC NEWTON

Sir Isaac Newton was an English scientist and mathematician. He studied optics, motion, and mathematics. In 1687, Newton published his most famous work, titled *Philosophiae Naturalis Principia Mathematica* (*Mathematical Principles of Natural Philosophy*). It was the first book of modern physics that explained how the physical world works.

In *Principia*, Newton described his three laws of motion. He also explained his theory of gravity, which states that the force of gravity affects all objects, even those beyond Earth. This helped to explain the movements of the planets and the sun.

Most objects move in predictable ways. For example, if you hold a spoon in your hand and let go of it, what happens? The spoon falls to the ground. It doesn't float sideways or up toward the clouds. When a classmate bumps into you in the school hallway, your body moves sideways. When a skateboard rolls across the driveway, it eventually stops. Each of these examples of motion can be explained by physics.

Sir Isaac Newton (1643–1727) was an English scientist who studied the motion of many physical objects. How and why do objects move? What makes an object stop moving? What happens when an outside force pushes or pulls an object? Newton answered these questions with his three laws of motion. These ideas became the foundation of modern physics.

NEWTON'S FIRST LAW OF MOTION

Newton's first law of motion states that an object at rest will remain at rest and an object in motion will stay in motion in a straight line at a constant speed unless it is acted upon by an outside force.

What does this mean? A bicycle isn't going to move unless someone pushes on the pedals and makes it go. And, once the bike is moving, it isn't going to stop or turn unless a force—such as the friction between tires and the road or someone applying the brakes or steering—halts or changes its motion.

An object at rest stays at rest

An object in motion stays in motion

An object in motion keeps moving because of inertia. All objects have inertia, whether they are at rest or are in motion.

If you want to push a full shopping cart, it takes some effort to get it moving. Yet, once the cart is moving, it takes less effort to keep it rolling over smooth ground. To stop the rolling cart, you'll need to use almost as much effort as you needed to start it. Why is it harder to start and stop the cart than it is to keep it moving? Inertia!

To change an object's motion, an unbalanced force must act on the object and overcome its inertia. The unbalanced force that acts on the shopping cart is the push you give it. Once the cart begins to move, inertia keeps it moving, even as friction slows it down. When you pull on the cart's handle, you create an unbalanced force that overcomes its inertia and the cart slows or stops moving.

An object's inertia depends on its mass. Mass is a measure of how much matter is in an object. An object with a greater mass has a greater inertia. Who would be easier to push on a skateboard, your 200-pound uncle or your 40-pound cousin? Your cousin has much less mass than your uncle and, therefore, has much less inertia to overcome. You would need a much smaller push—or force—to get the skateboard moving with your cousin on it. It would also be easier to stop your cousin than your uncle.

Newton's first law of motion is also known as the law of inertia. Inertia is an object's tendency to resist any change in its motion. Because of inertia, an object at rest stays at rest.

Take a look at this longboarder's journey down a curvy road. What forces is he using to stay upright? How does he change the direction of his board? What do his arms contribute?

Please remember this is a professional with a lot of experience. Don't try these moves at home!

Loaded Boards
Longboarding Let Go

Newton's first law of motion explains how and why a skateboard starts and stops rolling. A skateboard resting on the pavement will not move unless a force acts on it. To start the board rolling, a rider places one foot on the board and uses the other foot to push off the ground. This push generates a force that causes the skateboard to move.

Smooth sailing? But wait! At the same time, the force of friction pushes on the skateboard's wheels in the opposite direction of its motion. As long as the force of the skater's push is stronger than the force of friction, the skateboard continues to move forward. Once the skater stops pushing, the skateboard slows to a stop because of the friction opposing its motion.

Newton's first law of motion also explains how a skateboarder changes direction while riding. Once again, unbalanced forces come into play.

Under Newton's first law, an object in motion will remain in motion at the same speed and direction unless acted upon by an outside force.

A rolling skateboard continues to move at the same speed and in the same direction as long as no force acts on it. To change the board's direction, a skater can press down on one side of the skateboard. Pressing down on one side of the board creates an unbalanced force, which causes the skateboard to turn in the opposite direction.

NEWTON'S SECOND LAW OF MOTION

When an object moves, it has velocity. Velocity is the speed of an object in a certain direction. What happens when an object moves faster or slower? Its velocity changes. The change in an object's velocity is called acceleration. Because velocity is both speed and direction, acceleration can occur when an object changes speed, changes direction, or changes both.

What makes a moving skateboard, or any object, accelerate? Force! Acceleration occurs when an unbalanced force acts on an object. Acceleration of an object depends on two factors: the force acting on the object and the object's mass.

Newton explains this relationship in his second law of motion, known as the law of acceleration. When a force is applied to an object, that object will accelerate. How much an object accelerates depends on the strength of the outside force and on the object's mass.

GALILEO STUDIES MOTION

Before Newton, Italian philosopher and scientist Galileo Galilei (1564–1642) also studied motion. In some of his experiments, he observed the motion of objects as they rolled down varying inclines. When timing the motion, Galileo discovered the distance an object traveled was proportional to the square of its time in motion. These early experiments led to the first concept of acceleration.

FLIP FACT

Velocity is measured in meters per second (m/s), while acceleration is measured in meters per second squared (m/s^2).

Newton's second law states that an object's acceleration is equal to the net force acting on it divided by its mass. You can calculate acceleration (a) by dividing the net force (F) by the mass (m):

$$a = F \div m$$

Newton's second law shows that force and acceleration have a direct relationship. When one increases, the other also increases.

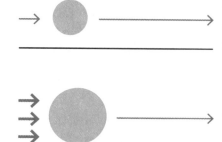

Objects with more mass require more force to move.

The greater the force applied to an object, the more the object accelerates. So, the harder you push your skateboard, the faster you go.

FLIP FACT

Let's compare how Newton's law of acceleration affects two skateboarders. Ava has a mass of 120 pounds, while her friend Mia has a mass of 90 pounds. If both girls push off on their skateboards with the same force, which one will have the greater acceleration? According to Newton's second law, mass and acceleration have an inverse relationship. With the same force, Mia, who has less mass, will have greater acceleration on her board. She will move faster than Ava.

In contrast, acceleration and mass have an inverse relationship. When one increases, the other decreases. Therefore, the greater an object's mass, the less it accelerates when the same size force acts on it. For example, if you push a skateboard carrying two of your friends (a greater mass), it accelerates less than when you push the board holding only one of your friends (less mass).

So, how does Newton's second law of motion affect skateboarding? To go faster, riders can push harder off the ground. This creates a greater force acting on the board. When force increases, acceleration also increases.

NEWTON'S THIRD LAW OF MOTION

Newton's third law of motion is called the law of action and reaction. This law states that every action has an equal and opposite reaction.

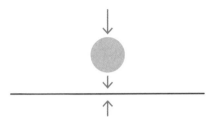

An object reacts to force with an equal and opposite reaction.

Have you ever blown up a balloon and then let it go without tying it? What happens? That balloon flying around the room is a great illustration of Newton's third law of motion!

In this example, the action is the release of air that flows downward from the balloon. The reaction occurs when the release of air—the action—causes the balloon to rise upward.

Since we know that every action has an equal and opposite reaction, we can see that forces always act in pairs. The reaction is equal in strength to the action, but acts in the opposite direction. In skateboarding, an action occurs when the skater pushes against the ground with their foot. The ground pushes back against the skater's foot, which is the equal and opposite reaction. This force starts the skateboard moving forward.

Space is a great place to test Newton's laws of motion! Take a look at the experiments in this video from the International Space Station.

Why do objects behave differently in a zero-gravity environment?

NASA
STEMonstration
third law

EQUILIBRIUM AND PHYSICS

In physics, an object is in a state of equilibrium when all the forces acting on that object are balanced. Forces are considered balanced if the forces pushing rightward are balanced by the forces pushing leftward and downward forces are balanced by upward forces. Equilibrium means the net force acting on the object equals zero. However, an object at equilibrium does not mean the object must be at rest. By following Newton's first law of motion, the object is either at rest and staying at rest or in motion and staying in motion at the same speed and direction. There is no acceleration.

If the skater pushes harder against the ground, with greater force, what happens? Because the action force is greater, the equal and opposite reaction force is also greater. The skater is pushed by the ground with more force, which causes the skateboard to move faster and farther.

Action and reaction forces are equal and opposite forces. Yet, because they act on different objects, they do not cancel each other out. They are not balanced forces. In most cases, action and reaction forces produce motion.

SKATEBOARDING WITH MOMENTUM

Have you ever noticed that some objects in motion are easier to stop than others? The difference is related to an object's momentum.

All moving objects have momentum, or mass in motion. Remember that all objects have mass. If an object is moving, its mass is in motion. That means that all moving objects have momentum. A moving object's momentum depends on two factors. These are its mass and its velocity, or the speed of an object in any direction.

You can calculate momentum (p) by multiplying mass (m) by velocity (v):

$$p = m \times v$$

The equation shows that momentum has a direct relationship to both mass and velocity. If mass increases, momentum increases. If velocity increases, momentum increases. A skateboard has more momentum when it is moving faster than when it is moving more slowly.

If two skateboarders roll down the street at the same velocity, the skateboarder with the greater mass has more momentum.

JUMPING THE OLLIE

What does all of this mean for skateboarders? Let's take a look at a trick.

The ollie is a trick that skaters use to jump onto curbs and over obstacles. As the skater jumps into the air, the skateboard also rises up and appears to be glued to the skater's feet. How can a skater get the board to jump into the air without holding on to it? It takes a little bit of physics (and practice)!

When a skater stands still on their board, three forces are acting on the skateboard.

- First, gravity pulls the board toward Earth.

- Second, the weight of the skater pushes down on the board.

- And third, the ground pushes up on the skateboard.

The net force of the three forces is zero. They all act on the same object—the skateboard—and balance each other out. The objects are in a state of equilibrium.

When skaters start their run, they push off the ground to start the board rolling. With no additional force to affect its movement, the skateboard continues to roll at a constant speed.

To jump, skaters crouch down and bend their knees. Then, they jump up explosively and straighten their knees. This creates a greater force that pushes down on the board and the ground (action).

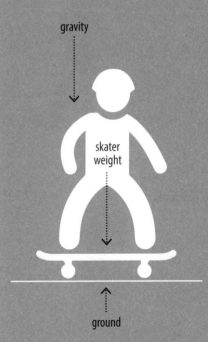

According to Newton's third law of motion, every action has an equal and opposite reaction. The ground pushes back on the skater with the same amount of force, which helps to accelerate them into the air.

At the same time, a force called torque affects the board. Torque is a force that rotates objects around a specific point, called a pivot point or an axis. During a jump, the skater's back foot pushes with much greater force on the back of the board than their front foot pushes on the front of the board.

This causes the back wheels to become a pivot point. The back of the board moves toward the ground, while the front of the board moves upward. When the board's tail hits the ground, the ground provides a large upward force on the tail.

The upward force causes the board to bounce up, completely in the air, with the front of the board angled higher than the back of the board.

As the skater slides their front foot forward, the sliding friction between their foot and the board drags the board upward even higher. The skater pushes their front foot with more force and lifts their rear leg slightly. This creates torque on the board again and the board pivots around its own center. This allows the board to level out in the air at its maximum height.

With practice, the skater can time this move so that their rear foot and the back of the board rise together. Board and foot appear stuck together. Then, gravity pulls the skater and board back to Earth.

THE HIPPIE JUMP

Another skateboarding trick is the hippie jump. Once again, forces are at play! First, skateboarders roll along a flat horizontal surface on their boards.

Watch this video of an ollie.

Remember to wear a helmet if you ever ride a skateboard!

SciShow ollie

They jump up and briefly fly through the air as the boards roll on the ground below. Then, they land back on the boards and continue moving along. What role does physics have in the hippie jump?

A skateboarder riding on a skateboard travels at a certain velocity. Remember, velocity is an object's speed in a certain direction. To perform the hippie jump, a skater jumps straight up by pushing down vertically with their legs, without exerting any horizontal force on the board. If they push on the board with any horizontal force, the board shifts ahead or behind.

Through the jump, the skater moves through the air at the same horizontal velocity as the board below. Because both the skater and the board are moving at the same horizontal velocity, the board remains beneath them. The force of friction acting on the board as it rolls along the surface is small enough that it does not slow the board enough to make a difference to the skater. The force of gravity pulls the skater back to the ground and they land on top of the board.

WORK IN PHYSICS

When a force acts on an object and moves the object from its place or position, work was done on the object. Work includes force and displacement. For a force to work on an object, the force must cause displacement by moving the object from its place or position. When you push a grocery cart, you perform work. When you throw a ball or lift a heavy backpack, you perform work.

Watch a video of a hippie jump.

What do skateboarders do to get their bodies ready to make a jump? How does this help?

Robertson action science hippie

Credit: James Alby (CC BY-ND 2.0)

In all these cases, a force acts on an object and causes the object to move or be displaced.

We've seen how skaters perform work (even though it looks like play!) as they pop ollies and hippie jumps. What are some other sports that require forces to be applied to different equipment? Well, the easy answer is all of them! Sports rely on physics to move baseballs, shoot basketballs, balance on a beam, and slice through the water during a swim race.

Another sport where you can really see how forces work is snowboarding! As with skateboarders, snowboarders rely on momentum, friction, gravity, and more to glide down a mountain or flip over a jump.

Let's take a look in the next chapter.

A scalar quantity is a quantity that is described only by its magnitude. Examples of scalar quantities include speed, mass, volume, temperature, power, energy, and time.

TEXT TO WORLD

What role do good shoes play in the sport of skateboarding? Why?

KEY QUESTIONS

- Have you ever ridden on a skateboard? What did it feel like? Were you able to find your balance?

- How do forces affect you when you're running up a hill? Sitting in your chair? Jumping from a diving board?

- How does a better understanding of physics help you become a better skateboarder? Is there a connection between what your brain knows and what your body practices?

Ideas for Supplies ▼

- round objects to use as wheels, such as bottle caps or empty tape rolls
- objects to make axles, such as pencils through a paper tube or wooden skewers through a straw
- materials such as cardboard or plastic for the skateboard's deck

TEST THE LAW OF ACCELERATION

Newton's second law of motion, the law of acceleration, explains the relationship between force, mass, and acceleration. It states that the net force on an object equals the object's mass multiplied by its acceleration.

$$F \text{ (net force)} = m \text{ (mass)} \times a \text{ (acceleration)}$$

In this activity, you'll build a mini skateboard and investigate how each variable affects the others.

- **Choose your materials and build a mini skateboard.** Create axles to hold the wheels so they can rotate. Try to construct the skateboard so that its motion is smooth. It needs to be sturdy enough to be handled repeatedly without falling apart.

- **Explore how force affects acceleration.** Give the skateboard a light push across a level surface. Use a measuring tape or stick to measure how far the skateboard travels from its starting point to where it comes to a complete stop. Use a timer or stopwatch to measure the time it takes for the skateboard to travel this distance. Record the results in your science journal.

- **Calculate the skateboard's average velocity using the following equation.**

    average velocity = total distance in meters ÷ total time in seconds

- **Calculate acceleration using the following equations.** First, you'll need to find your initial and final velocity. You can use average velocity to do this.

    average velocity = (final velocity + initial velocity) ÷ 2

- **In this example, we'll use an average velocity of 10 m/s.** You can use the average velocity you calculated in the previous step. We'll also assume initial velocity is 0. We can solve this equation for final velocity, then calculate acceleration.

$$10 \text{ m/s} = (Fv + 0) \div 2$$

$$20 \text{ m/s} = Fv + 0$$

$$20 \text{ m/s} = Fv$$

Acceleration = (final velocity - initial velocity) ÷ time elapsed in seconds

- **Repeat the process and calculations, changing the force used to push the skateboard.** Try a medium push and a hard push. Record your results.

- **Use the data you have collected to create a graph or chart of your results.** What do your results show about the relationship between force, mass, and acceleration?

	DISTANCE	TIME	AVERAGE VELOCITY	ACCELERATION
EASY				
MEDIUM				
HARD				

To investigate more, try changing the mass in your experiment. How can you change the mass of the skateboard? Try to keep the pushing force constant but change the skateboard's mass and repeat the experiment. What happens?

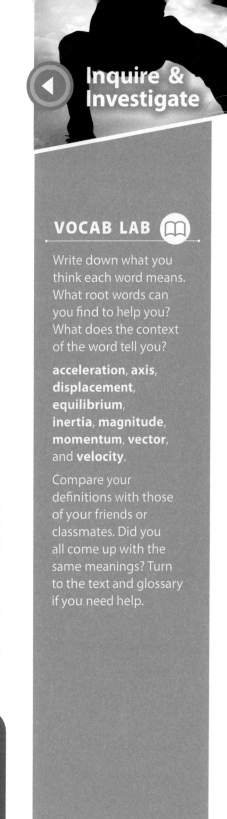

VOCAB LAB 📖

Write down what you think each word means. What root words can you find to help you? What does the context of the word tell you?

acceleration, **axis**, **displacement**, **equilibrium**, **inertia**, **magnitude**, **momentum**, **vector**, and **velocity**.

Compare your definitions with those of your friends or classmates. Did you all come up with the same meanings? Turn to the text and glossary if you need help.

Ideas for Supplies ▼

- 2 PVC pipes, one with a smaller diameter so that it fits easily inside the other
- small hacksaw
- sandpaper
- drill
- paper clip
- thick rubber band
- 2 small metal washers
- wire

MAKE A FORCE METER

A force is a push or pull on an object when it interacts with another object. Forces cause an object to move or stop moving. They can also make an object stay still. Forces are measured in units called newtons (N). Scientists use force meters to measure the size of a force. In this activity, you'll make your own simple force meter.

Find diagrams and more information on building a force meter at this website.

CAUTION: Ask an adult for help with this project.

Instructables
force meter

- **Cut an 8-inch piece from the smaller PVC pipe and cut a 2-inch piece from the wider pipe.** Use sandpaper to smooth the cut edges on each pipe piece.

- **In the wider pipe, drill two holes opposite each other near one end of the pipe.** In the narrower pipe, drill four evenly spaced holes around one end. These holes need to be large enough to thread a rubber band through them. Use sandpaper to smooth the edges around each drilled hole.

- **Put the smaller pipe inside the larger one.** Line up the outer holes with two of the inner holes.

- **Thread the rubber band through the holes so that it stretches through both the outer and inner pipes in a line.** You may need to use a paperclip or small wire (straightened and bent in half) to help thread the rubber band through the holes.

- **Push each end of the rubber band through the middle of a metal washer.** Bring the band back outside the washer to secure it to the band.

- **Add a loop to the force meter by threading the wire through the two unused holes in the inner pipe.** You can do this by pulling the outer pipe down to expose the extra holes in the inner pipe. Tie the ends of the wire together to secure the loop. Add a piece of masking tape to the outside of the inner pipe.

- **Calibrate the force meter by holding the force meter upright by the outer pipe and marking the tape.** The bottom edge of the outer pipe is the meter's zero point, so label it "0N" (newtons).

- **Continue to calibrate by hanging an object with 100 grams of mass off the loop.** A mass of 100 grams weighs approximately 1 newton. Mark the tape on the force meter as 1 newton. Repeat the process with objects with other known masses (50 grams, 200 grams, 300 grams) and mark the tape for each and label with newtons (0.5N, 2N, 3N, etc.) Using objects with known masses, complete the measurement scale on the force meter and extend it to the edge of the smaller pipe. What is the largest force your force meter can measure?

- **Once the force meter is calibrated, use it to measure a variety of objects.** Holding the meter by the outside pipe, hang objects from the loop to find the weight. Attach a hook to the loop and you can measure the force needed to move an object. If you turn the meter around and hold it by the outer pipe, you can use the inner pipe to measure the force needed to push an object.

Inquire & Investigate

To investigate more, design an experiment using the force meter to test the effects of known forces. You might investigate how far an object will move if pushed with a force of x newtons or another experiment of your choosing!

EXPLORING INERTIA

Inertia is an object's tendency to resist any change in its motion. Because of inertia, an object at rest stays at rest and an object in motion keeps moving. All objects have inertia, whether they are at rest or are in motion. In this activity, you'll explore how inertia keeps an object moving.

CAUTION: Always wear a helmet on a skateboard.

- **Gather three volunteers who are happy to share their weight and sit on a skateboard while pushed.** Assign each a job to start. One will sit on the skateboard, another will run the timer, and a third will push the skateboard.

- **Using a medium-sized push, set the skateboard with the volunteer sitting on it in motion.** Time how long the skateboard remains in motion. Once it stops, measure how far it moved from start to finish. Create a chart with the following data: weight of rider, time elapsed, distance traveled, and size of push.

- **Repeat this process with the same person on the skateboard but vary the size of the push.** Record your data.

- **Change the volunteer on the skateboard.** Repeat the process several times with small-, medium-, and large-sized pushes. Be careful that your pushes are not too hard or reckless. Repeat again with a third volunteer rider. Record your data each time.

- **Analyze the data you collected.** What does it tell you about Newton's first law of motion? How does inertia affect the skateboard during this experiment? Create a visual presentation to share what you have learned.

To investigate more, put a small object (such as a stuffed animal or block) on the skateboard and push the skateboard in motion toward an obstacle such as a wall or step. What happens when the skateboard runs into the obstacle? What happens to the object riding on the skateboard? How does Newton's first law of motion explain what happened?

Chapter 2

Motion and Energy of Snowboarding

IT'S ALL DOWNHILL FROM HERE!

How do snowboarders get high in the air?

GRAVITY IS WHAT PULLS YOU AND YOUR BOARD DOWN THE SLOPES!

AND FRICTION HELPS DETERMINE HOW FAST YOU GET TO GO.

WITH SOME KNOWLEDGE OF PHYSICS, YOU CAN FLY!

Just as physics dictates how skateboards move, physics are also a big part of snowboarding! Gliding down mountain trails on a snowboard is a lesson in air resistance, acceleration, and gravity!

Snow is falling and you're excited to get out on the mountain. You grab your snowboard and make your way to the trail for some freestyle riding. Snowboarders race down slopes, carve turns in the snow, and soar so high they can rotate in the air.

To accomplish these incredible tricks, snowboarders rely on science. They use the laws of gravity to build speed and stay balanced on their boards. They also use physics to gain height in jumps.

As you glide across the snow, you are sliding over a thin layer of water. Friction between your board and the snow melts the snow and creates the water layer. As you ride, you shift your position to maintain your balance. You might not know it, but every shift helps you keep your center of gravity over the board.

Let's take a closer look at how it works!

GRAVITY: PULLING YOU DOWN THE MOUNTAIN

A snowboarder stands at the top of the hill. How do they shift from standing to moving?

We already know from the last chapter that, according to Newton's first law of motion (the law of inertia), an object will stay at rest until a force acts on it. In this case, the object is the snowboard with the snowboarder on it. The snowboarder creates the force needed to overcome inertia and move the board by pushing off the ground with their back foot.

FLIP FACT

Fresh powdered snow creates more friction than packed snow, slowing a snowboarder.

Newton's first law of motion also explains that, once the snowboard begins to move, it will keep moving unless another force acts on it to stop the motion.

One force that acts on snowboarders as they race down the mountain is gravity. Remember, gravity is a force of attraction that pulls two objects with mass toward each other. Earth's powerful gravity pulls everything on it, or near it, toward Earth's center.

Gravity's downward pull makes snowboarding possible. It gives snowboarders speed as they race down a mountain. After starting at the mountain's top, snowboarders rely entirely on gravity to generate their forward motion down the slope.

Long ago, people described objects in motion as either fast or slow. Galileo Galilei, the astronomer and mathematician, was the first to measure speed by using distance covered during a period of time, such as miles per hour.

Gravity also affects how snowboarders balance on their boards. On Earth, an object's center of gravity is located where the object's mass is concentrated. For humans, this point is generally found in the center of the body. To keep their balance, a snowboarder must keep their center of gravity over the board. If their center of gravity moves beyond the board, they are more likely to fall.

At the 2018 Winter Olympics in PyeongChang, China, the snowboard ramp was the biggest in the world, measuring about 160 feet tall. A fall from that height is extremely dangerous. So, how do snowboarders fly off the ramp, perform tricks, and land safely?

The key is the ramp's design. Like many snow ramps, the PyeongChang ramp was designed with a downward slope for riders to land on. When snowboarders land at an angle and continue moving down a slope, the impact on them is the same as if they had fallen from a much lower height.

Some of the snowboarders' gravitational potential energy gets converted into forward-moving kinetic energy.

FLIP FACT

When a slope is not steep, gravity has less of an effect on a snowboarder's speed. On steep slopes, gravity has a much greater effect.

Because of the conversion to kinetic energy, their bodies have less energy to absorb upon impact. This reduces the potential for injury.

Gravitational potential energy is the energy stored in an object because of its vertical position or height. The energy is stored because of gravity's downward pull on the object toward Earth. The higher the object is off the ground, the greater gravity's downward pull on it and the more gravitational potential energy it has.

FRICTION ON THE SLOPE

The force of gravity pulls snowboarders down a slope and gives them speed. Going fast down a mountain can be exhilarating. Going too fast can be dangerous! A snowboarder who goes too fast might lose control. That's why snowboarders use friction to slow down and control their rides.

As we learned in the last chapter, friction is a force that acts when two objects move against each other.

When a snowboard slides over snow, it creates friction between the snow and the snowboard, slowing its motion down the mountain.

That friction also produces heat, which melts the top layer of snow so the snowboard glides along the surface of the water instead of the surface of the snow. This reduces the amount of friction and lets the snowboard move faster. Snowboarders also use wax on their boards to reduce friction between the board and the snow.

Snowboarders must find a good balance between too much friction and too little friction.

Gravitational potential energy depends on two factors: mass and height. The more mass an object has, the greater its gravitational potential energy. Similarly, the higher the object is above the ground, the greater its gravitational potential energy.

A racing snowboard is made to be skinny and lightweight to reduce friction and allow snowboarders to ride faster down the mountain.

This balance keeps their speed exactly right. Without friction, the snow could become too slippery, and the snowboarder could lose control.

To reduce speed and increase control, snowboarders often move back and forth across a slope in a zig-zag pattern. This back-and-forth motion increases the friction between the board and the snow. As friction increases, the board slows down, and the snowboarder maintains better control over the ride.

USING PHYSICS FOR TURNS AND CONTROL

Amateur snowboarders often skid when they try to turn. The snowboard tilts on its edge and the base of the board acts as a plow in the snow. Although the snowboarder might be able to control the skid and complete the turn, skidding causes the snowboarder to lose a lot of speed. The board's plowing action creates frictional resistance with the snow, which slows the snowboard's motion.

In most turns, some skidding occurs, but **the less skidding, the less speed is lost** during the turn.

To maintain speed while turning, experienced snowboarders execute a carved turn. In a carved turn, the board's hard metal edges cut through the snow like a carving knife. The snowboarders dig into the snow with the edges of their snowboards and lean into the direction they want to move.

The result is less snow resistance and less loss of speed, so the snowboarder can ride the course faster. Executing a carved turn takes a lot of skill.

AIR RESISTANCE

Another force that impacts snowboarding is air resistance. This type of friction is a force that pushes against an object when it moves through air. As snowboarders ride down the slope, air resistance pushes against their bodies and slows their speed.

As snowboarders ride down the mountain, gravity pulls them down, while air resistance and friction push against their motion. When gravity is stronger than air resistance and friction, the net force on snowboarders causes them to accelerate and move faster.

Take a look at this slow-motion, first-person video!

What forces are at play as they glide down the mountain?

Nomad Press snowboarding video

At some point, the forces of air resistance, friction, and gravity balance each other out.

When the forces are balanced, snowboarders reach terminal velocity. At terminal velocity, snowboarders are moving at their maximum speeds and will not move any faster.

Air resistance is why parachutes work. The parachute greatly increases the amount of resistance a body will experience while falling through the air, meaning that the sky diver will reach the ground safely!

POSITION, SPEED, AND ACCELERATION

In physics, motion occurs when an object changes its position as time passes. An object's motion can be described by its position, speed, direction, and acceleration.

All motion is relative. An object is in motion when its position relative to another object changes. Whether an object is moving or not depends on your point of view. Think about a man riding in a train. The man is not moving in relation to his seat. He is, however, moving in relation to the trees that the train passes.

An object is in motion if it changes position compared to a reference point, which is an object or place used to determine if an object is in motion.

When snowboarders crouch down, they can become more aerodynamic, which means they can reduce air resistance and move more easily through the air.

In our example, the tree is a reference point to determine that the man on the train is in motion. Generally, a reference point is stationary.

Speed is another way to describe motion. The speed of an object is the distance it moves during one unit of time. When in motion, is the snowboarder moving fast or slow? What is the distance the snowboarder travels in a specific unit of time? Speed equals the distance traveled by the amount of time used to travel that distance. It is measured in miles per hour (mph or m/h) or meters per second (m/s). You can calculate the snowboarder's speed in this way.

$$distance \div time = speed$$

For example, a snowboarder travels 5 miles down a hill in 15 minutes (0.25 hour).

$$5\ miles \div 0.25\ hour = 20\ miles\ per\ hour$$

Motion also has direction. An object's speed describes how fast it is moving but does not describe the direction of its motion. Is the object moving left or right, up or down? Perhaps a snowboarder is riding down the hill in a zig-zag pattern, changing direction repeatedly.

When you know an object's speed and direction, you can determine its velocity.

Velocity is the speed in a given direction. A snowboarder's speed could be 20 miles per hour, but the velocity would be 20 miles per hour in a southeast direction.

WAXING THE BOARD

Snowboarders apply wax to the bottom of their boards to improve how the board moves on snow. The wax reduces the friction between the board and the snow. Reducing the friction gives the snowboarder a smoother ride and allows the boarder to fly down the mountain faster.

FLIP FACT

The average snowboarder rides at speeds of 20 to 30 miles per hour. An Olympic snowboarder can reach speeds of up to 70 miles per hour.

AVERAGE SPEED

Most objects do not move at a constant speed. They travel a little faster or a little slower. When you ride your bike, your speed varies as you go up and down hills, stop at a traffic light, slow down for kids crossing the road, and lots of other reasons. Instead of noting all the different speeds during this bike ride, you can figure out the average speed.

The average speed of an object is equal to the total distance traveled divided by the total time spent (total distance ÷ total time = average speed). If you bike 5 miles in half an hour, your average speed is 5 miles ÷ 0.5 hour or 10 miles per hour.

When snowboarders ride down the hill, they speed up and slow down at different points. Their velocity changes. Velocity can change in three ways. An object can speed up, slow down, or change directions. As we learned in the last chapter, acceleration is the rate of change in an object's velocity. You might think that only speeding up is acceleration, but so is slowing down and changing direction.

You can calculate an object's acceleration by subtracting the original velocity from the final velocity and dividing the result by time.

**acceleration =
(final velocity – original velocity) ÷ time**

For example, a snowboarder rides down a short slope. Her initial velocity is 5 meters per second (m/s). After 8 seconds, her velocity is 15 m/s. What is her acceleration?

**acceleration = (15 m/s – 5 m/s) ÷ 8 seconds
acceleration = 1.25 m/s²**

Remember that velocity is measured in meters per second (m/s), while acceleration is measured in meters per second squared (m/s²).

GRAVITY IN THE HALF-PIPE

Sometimes, snowboarders race down the mountain. Other times, they ride through a half-pipe, where they can perform jumps and tricks. A snowboarding half-pipe is a U-shaped ramp or runway with high sides in the snow. It looks just like its name, as if someone removed the top half of a round pipe, leaving the bottom half in the snow.

To ride in the half-pipe, snowboarders use the principles of gravity, speed, friction, and balance. They start at the top of the half-pipe and ride straight over the snow, using gravity to gain speed. Friction and air resistance also affect the snowboarder during the run, slowing down the motion of the board. If they have enough speed when their snowboard reaches the top edge, the snowboarder flies into the air.

Gravity then pulls the snowboarder back down to the pipe.

They ride down the pipe's side and return to the center, gaining enough momentum to ride up the other side of the half-pipe and repeat the process. When a rider is in the air, they must keep their center of gravity over the board or else they will fall.

KINETIC AND POTENTIAL ENERGY

If you've ever strapped on a snowboard, you know that it takes a lot of energy to ride down a mountain or through a half-pipe. Energy is key. In physics, energy is what gives objects the ability to move and change. Energy can be stored and measured in several forms, such as heat, motion, light, chemicals, and sound.

While energy comes in different forms, all energy falls into one of two categories: kinetic energy or potential energy.

Kinetic energy is measured in units called joules (J). An object's kinetic energy (KE) is equal to half of its mass (m) multiplied by its velocity (v) squared, as written in this equation.

$$KE = \tfrac{1}{2}m \times v^2$$

What can we learn about the relationship between kinetic energy, mass, and velocity from this equation? First, the equation shows that kinetic energy is directly proportional to an object's mass. If the mass of an object increases, kinetic energy also increases. The equation also shows that an increase in velocity causes a much greater increase in kinetic energy.

Imagine two snowboarders riding down a mountain. Both have approximately the same mass. If one snowboarder moves twice as fast as the second snowboarder, what happens to the kinetic energy of each? The first snowboarder has four times as much kinetic energy as the second snowboarder.

FLIP FACT

Kinetic energy is the energy of motion. Any time an object is moving, it has kinetic energy. The amount of kinetic energy of an object depends on two factors: the object's mass and its speed, or velocity.

Potential energy is the energy stored in an object because of its position. When you are resting and not moving, your body has potential energy.

Imagine a snowboarder at the top of a mountain, not yet moving. All the snowboarder's potential energy is stored in their body. When they start moving, the potential energy is released and becomes kinetic energy—energy in motion.

How are potential and kinetic energy related? The two types of energy depend on each other. Kinetic energy exists only when stored energy—potential energy—is released. And potential energy stores kinetic energy in any object, including your body.

ENERGY ON THE MOUNTAIN

On the mountain, snowboarders move between potential and kinetic energy. At the start, the motionless snowboarders are full of potential energy. As they ride down the slope, they convert potential energy into kinetic energy. Not all the potential energy converts into kinetic energy, however.

Some potential energy is converted into heat, or thermal energy, as the snowboards cut through the snow and create friction. Some is used against air resistance as snowboarders push against the air.

Watch Olympic snowboarder Shaun White perform in the 2018 Olympics.

Where do you see gravity, friction, and air resistance at work?

Shaun White 2018
half-pipe gold

Kinetic energy depends on the mass of an object and its speed, or velocity.

To jump higher in the half-pipe, a lighter snowboarder needs to generate more speed than a heavier snowboarder.

When snowboarders ride up the side of the half-pipe, they have kinetic energy and move fast. When they soar into the air at the top, they slow down. And when snowboarders reach the highest points in the air, their speed drops to zero. For a split second, they are not moving and appear to hang in the air. At that point, all of the snowboarders' kinetic energy has been converted into potential energy.

But gravity makes quick work of that potential energy! Gravity pulls the snowboarders back down to the pipe. As they move down the side of the half-pipe, their potential energy decreases and kinetic energy increases. At the bottom of the half-pipe, all the potential energy has been turned into kinetic energy (plus some thermal energy). As snowboarders ride up the other side of the half-pipe, the energy cycle repeats itself.

PUMPING ON A HALF-PIPE

Pumping is a technique that snowboarders use on a half-pipe to increase their speed as they reach the top of the pipe's side. The faster they are riding, the higher they can fly in the air above the pipe.

With more height, they can perform more aerial tricks!

To increase speed, snowboarders learn to add energy to their snowboarding system. In physics, a system is an organized collection of parts that work together to achieve a goal. In snowboarding, the system includes the snowboarder, the snowboard, and the ground.

To increase speed, snowboarders keep their feet firmly on the snowboard. They crouch down in the straight, center part of the half-pipe. When they begin to move up the curved pipe side, the snowboarders quickly lift their bodies and arms up. This motion adds kinetic energy to the system. Increased kinetic energy allows the snowboarders to exit the pipe at a greater speed and fly higher in the air.

The process of pumping on a snowboard adds energy to the system in the same way as pumping your legs on a swing adds energy and makes you go higher.

AERIAL TRICKS

Some snowboarders perform aerial tricks when they fly into the air. They perform spins, twists, and grab their boards. How can they do this? You guessed it: physics! The main physics principle involved in every spin and twist is the conservation of angular momentum.

As we learned in the last chapter, momentum is mass in motion. Typically, this motion is linear, or in a straight line. Some objects, however, spin around like a top instead of moving in a straight line. Spinning objects have angular momentum.

Angular momentum depends on how spread out the object is and how fast it is moving. The more mass and velocity the object has, the greater its angular momentum and the more difficult it is to stop or change direction. Angular momentum is calculated by multiplying the object's mass by its velocity and its radius.

THE GRANDFATHER OF SNOWBOARDING

On Christmas morning in 1965, an engineer named Sherman Poppen (1930–2019) fastened two skis together. He took them to the top of a snowy backyard hill and rode them down. This first board became known as a "snurfer" because it combined snow and surfing. A few weeks later, Poppen added a rope to the board's front to make it easier for the rider to turn and prevent it from sliding away when the rider fell. Poppen patented his idea and licensed it to a manufacturer. During the next 15 years, Poppen's "snurfer" became a hit and sold more than 750,000 boards. Poppen became known as the grandfather of snowboarding and inspired a generation of athletes to try surfing on snow.

A rotating stool is a great place to learn about the conservation of angular momentum. Take a look at this video!

What happens when the amount of weight is increased?

NCSSM rotating stool

In physics, conservation of momentum means that a system cannot lose momentum—momentum must always go somewhere. In a closed system with no impact from outside forces, momentum stays the same, or constant. If one factor changes, the others must also change for the momentum to remain the same.

Due to the conservation of angular momentum, any object that spins around an axis continues to spin at the same velocity until something gets in its way or the object changes its shape.

If the radius of an object decreases, its velocity must increase to keep angular momentum constant.

Have you ever been on a swing that's twisted up and spins when you release it? What happens when you put your arms and feet out? What if you pull them in to make your body tighter? You slow down and speed up, right? This is due to the conservation of angular momentum.

When snowboarders pull in their arms and reduce how spread out they are, their spinning speed must increase to keep angular momentum the same. In the same way, a spinning figure skater will spin faster when they pull in their arms.

For aerial tricks, snowboarders rotate their bodies upon takeoff. This gives them angular momentum. In the air, the snowboarders can change their body shapes and arm positions to create a display of aerial tricks. The entire time, their angular momentum remains the same.

The force of gravity, along with kinetic and potential energies, is also at work on a trampoline! Just like snowboarding, jumping on a trampoline depends on gravity and energy to fly high in the air.

Let's investigate how it works in the next chapter.

Some snowboarders compete in big air competitions. They glide down a slope or ramp, launch into the air, and perform tricks. While in the air, they twist, spin, and grab their boards before they land back on the snow. To complete many of these tricks, snowboarders must have torque. Torque is a force that causes an object to rotate around an imaginary straight line called an axis. Torque causes a snowboarder's body to rotate around a vertical axis in the air. To create torque, snowboarders twist their bodies in the opposite direction of how they want to spin. This increases the number of times that the snowboarders can spin.

You can see some big air action in the video in this article!

2020/21 FIS

KEY QUESTIONS

- **How are snowboarding and skateboarding similar in terms of physics? How are they different?**
- **What effect might the quality of the snow have on a snowboarder's experience?**
- **How do the laws of physics apply to skiing? Is it different from snowboarding?**

TEXT TO WORLD

How does gravity affect the sport of basketball? Diving? Dancing?

To investigate more, design a variation of this experiment that adds friction, air resistance, or another force that resists the pull of gravity. How does this affect the motion of your objects?

THE FORCE OF GRAVITY

Every time you fall or you drop an object to the ground, you're experiencing gravity. Gravity is a force that pulls two objects with mass toward each other. Earth's gravity pulls you toward its center. And gravity pulls snowboarders down the mountain. In this activity, you'll explore the force of gravity and how it affects the motion of objects.

- **Create a simple inclined plane using a stack of books and a piece of plywood.** Measure the height of the plane and record it in your science journal.

- **Select an object and place it at the top of the ramp.** Release it and time how long it takes to roll down the ramp. Record your data, including the height of the plane, type of object, object weight, and time to roll down ramp.

- **Repeat this procedure with different objects.** Record your data for each attempt.

- **Try varying the height of the plane by adding or removing books.** Send each of your objects down the ramp again and record your data.

- **Analyze the data.** These may be helpful questions.

  - Which objects rolled the fastest down the plane? Which rolled the slowest? How do you explain these results?

  - What happened when you changed the height of the plane?

  - How did the force of gravity affect the motion of the objects?

UPS AND DOWNS OF KINETIC AND POTENTIAL ENERGY

Snowboarders rely on gravitational potential energy and kinetic energy to race down the mountain! These work together to result in motion that is beautiful and fun. In this activity, you will investigate the relationship between kinetic and potential energy by building a marble roller coaster.

Ideas for Supplies ▼

- foam pipe insulation about 1½ inches in diameter and at least 6 feet long
- marble or small heavy ball

- **Carefully cut the pipe insulation in half lengthwise so that you have two long, U-shaped pieces.** Use the pipe insulation to create a roller coaster track. Get creative with the track and incorporate hills, turns, and a loop.

- **Tape one end of the track to a tabletop to create a large downward slope leading to the rest of the course.** Take a marble or small heavy ball and place it a few inches above the bottom of the first slope. When you let it go, how far does it make it through the course?

- **Move the marble a few inches higher on the first slope and release it.** Now how far does it go through the track? Record your observations in your science journal.

- **Repeat this process until you are releasing the marble at the tabletop.** Can the marble make it all the way through the track? How high does the initial slope need to be for the marble to make it through the entire track? If you start the marble from a higher point, what does that mean about its energy? Where does the marble move the fastest on the course? Where does it move the slowest? Can you explain why this happens? How is energy changing as the marble moves through the track?

> To investigate more, add another piece of pipe insulation at the end of the course that is level and straight. How far does the marble roll before it stops? What causes the marble to stop?

Chapter 3 ▶
Spring of a Trampoline

DEFYING GRAVITY IS A BREEZE!

What makes a trampoline so bouncy?

The stretchy surface of a trampoline and the springs that hold that surface to the frame give trampolines the bounce that sends you flying! Of course, the laws of physics are at work, too.

Have you ever jumped on a trampoline? Your feet hit the stretchy surface and your body launches several feet into the air. As you bounce up and down, you might even try a few tricks, such as jumps, flips, and spins. You can jump a lot higher on a trampoline than you can jump on the ground. Let's take a look at the laws of physics and how they explain the bounciness of a trampoline.

Jumping on a trampoline is a classic example of Newton's laws of motion. Newton's first law states that an object at rest will stay at rest until acted on by an outside force. If you do not exert an outside force by jumping on the trampoline, you stay at rest and do not bounce at all!

Newton's second law, the law of acceleration, explains how the upward acceleration you experience as you bounce is produced by a force acting on an object. In this case, the object is you, the jumper.

Newton's third law of motion states that for every action, there is an equal and opposite reaction. When you jump on a trampoline, action and reaction forces are at work. Every time you land on the trampoline and push down on its surface, you create an action force. An equal and opposite reaction force pushes back and lifts you up in the air.

And don't forget about the force of gravity! When you are on a trampoline, the force of gravity pulls you toward the ground.

POTENTIAL AND KINETIC ENERGY ON A TRAMPOLINE

Bouncing on a trampoline requires a lot of energy. In physics, energy on a trampoline takes the form of potential energy (stored energy) and kinetic energy (energy of motion). When you jump on a trampoline, you are part of a system that also includes the trampoline. As we learned earlier, a system is an organized collection of parts that work together to achieve a goal.

In physics, the law of conservation of energy states that energy cannot be created or destroyed. Instead, energy is converted from one form into another form. As a result, a closed system—one that has no outside forces affecting it—will always have the same amount of energy. On a trampoline, kinetic energy converts to potential energy and vice versa as you jump up and down. The total energy in the system remains the same.

FORMS OF KINETIC ENERGY

Kinetic energy is the energy of motion. Motion takes many forms, so there are different forms of kinetic energy. Vibrational kinetic energy is the energy created by vibrational motion, while rotational kinetic energy is the energy created by rotational motion. Translational kinetic energy is the energy created by motion from one location to another. On a trampoline, you have translational kinetic energy as you jump up and down.

FLIP FACT

Kinetic energy is a scalar quantity, which means it has only a magnitude and no direction.

But where does that energy come from? How does the trampoline system get energy to start?

When you first jump on a trampoline, the force of your body transfers energy into the system.

When you land on the trampoline mat and it stretches, potential energy is stored in the system.

When the trampoline snaps back to its original shape, it creates an upward force on you. It transfers potential energy to you in the form of kinetic energy that causes you to bounce up. As you bounce higher and faster, your kinetic energy increases.

When you are in the air, gravity pulls downward on you. As you come down from the peak of a jump, the force of gravity causes your velocity to increase. As velocity increases, more potential energy becomes kinetic energy, and you move faster as you approach the trampoline's surface.

Kinetic energy is greatest during the moment before you hit the trampoline surface and the moment when you leave the trampoline on your way back up into the air.

As you jump up, your velocity slows as gravity pulls downward on you. Plus, you also experience some air resistance. As your velocity slows, kinetic energy converts to potential energy. When you reach the peak of a jump, potential energy is at its maximum. The higher you jump, the more potential energy you have. As you fall again, your potential energy converts to kinetic energy and the cycle continues.

ELASTIC COLLISIONS

When two objects collide, momentum can sometimes transfer from one object to the other. Collisions can be elastic or inelastic—either the objects bounce off each other or they do not. In a closed system with no outside forces acting on the two objects, both elastic and inelastic collisions follow the law of conservation of momentum, which means no momentum is lost in the system.

In an elastic collision, kinetic energy is also conserved. The system's total kinetic energy remains almost the same before and after the collision. Think of a bouncy ball. When you drop the ball, it bounces off the pavement almost back to the height where it was dropped. Some kinetic energy is lost as heat energy, so the ball doesn't quite reach its original height.

Jumping on a trampoline is another example of an elastic collision.

In an inelastic collision, momentum is conserved, but kinetic energy is not. When the objects collide, some kinetic energy transfers to another type of energy, such as heat energy. When you drop a ball of clay, it splats on the floor with no bounce. All its energy is used to transform the ball into a blob on the floor.

Watch some world-class trampolining from the 2016 Olympics!

What do you notice about how the energy transfers from body to trampoline and back?

Olympics 2016 Trampoline Final

A trampoline's jumping mat is typically made from artificial fibers such as polyethylene and nylon. The fibers are tightly woven to create a webbed fabric. The fabric is strong enough to hold up to the stress and constant flexing of jumpers.

....

A fully elastic collision is rare. Usually, some kinetic energy is converted to sound or heat energy. For example, when you jump on a trampoline, the surface stretches and generates a little bit of heat energy.

TRAMPOLINE SPRINGS

What makes you bounce so high on a trampoline? Springs! A trampoline's surface is stretched and attached to several springs that connect to a rigid frame. A spring is a tightly wound spiral or coil of metal that stretches when pulled—or when a force is applied. A spring goes back to its original shape when it is released—or when the force is removed.

Objects that can stretch and then return to their original shape without being deformed are called elastic. A spring is elastic because it lengthens when a force is applied and returns to its original length when the force is removed.

A spring can also work in the opposite way. If squeezed by a force, it compresses and shortens. When the force is removed, the spring rebounds to its original length.

Springs can store elastic potential energy.

Elastic potential energy is a form of potential energy that is stored in elastic materials when they stretch or compress. Elastic potential energy can be stored in springs, rubber bands, bungee cords, and other stretchy materials. The amount of elastic potential energy stored in an object depends on the amount of stretch in the object. The more it stretches, the more elastic potential energy it stores.

Springs store elastic potential energy when they are stretched or compressed by a force.

The more the stretch or compression, the greater the force needed to stretch or compress the spring further. For some springs, the amount of force applied is directly proportional to the amount of stretch or compression.

A spring that is not stretched or compressed is in its equilibrium position. This is the spring's natural position with no force applied to it. In this position, a spring has no elastic potential energy.

Many springs used in machines are made from tough materials that can withstand being stretched many times without breaking. Stainless steel, bronze, and other tough alloys are common materials for springs.

This spring is in its equilibrium state.

HOOKE'S LAW

A British philosopher and scientist named Robert Hooke (1635–1703) studied the behavior of elastic materials during the seventeenth century. In his work, Hooke attempted to show the relationship between the forces applied to a spring and its elasticity. He developed a theory of elasticity, which is known as Hooke's law.

Hooke's law states that the force needed to stretch or compress a spring by some distance is proportional to that distance. In simpler terms, the force needed to stretch a spring is directly proportional to the amount of stretch that occurs. The stronger the force, the greater the stretch.

Hooke's law can be stated in the following equation: force applied = negative spring constant × displacement of the spring.

$$F = k \times X$$

In this equation, the spring constant (k) measures how stiff the spring is, while the displacement of the spring (X) is the distance the spring is stretched or compressed. According to this relationship, it takes twice as much force (F) to stretch a spring twice as far (X).

Hooke's law was one of the first explanations of the concept of elasticity, the property that allows an object to return to its original shape after being distorted. It applies to more than springs. Hooke's law applies any time an elastic object is deformed—for example, when you stretch a rubber band or inflate a balloon.

> In physics, conservation means something that does not change.

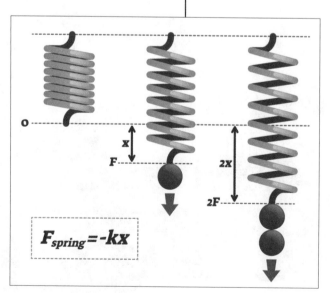

$F_{spring} = -kx$

Hooke's law does have some limitations. What happens when you stretch a rubber band too far? It snaps! No material can be stretched beyond a maximum amount or compressed more than a certain minimum size without becoming permanently deformed.

If you keep stretching beyond the maximum point—also known as the elastic limit— you'll stretch the object so far that it won't go back to its original length or form. It is permanently deformed. Have you ever blown up a balloon until it popped?

As long as a spring stays within its elastic limit, Hooke's law applies, but **if you stretch the spring too far past its elastic limit, it loses its stretchy quality.**

HOOKE'S LAW AND TRAMPOLINES

What does Hooke's law mean on a trampoline? When you land on the trampoline surface, you exert a force on the trampoline's springs, which causes them to stretch. The heavier you are, the greater the force and the more the trampoline's springs stretch.

Do you remember Newton's third law of motion, which states that every action has an equal and opposite reaction?

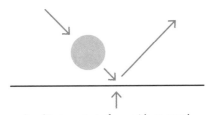

An object reacts to force with an equal and opposite reaction.

Listen to a scientific explanation of trampolining!

How does the whole body work to create spins?

Sheffield physics trampolining

Trampolines get their bounce from the interaction of Hooke's law with Newton's third law of motion. When you land on a trampoline's surface, you exert a force (action) on the springs, which stretches the surface and causes the springs to extend. The surface and springs try to return to their original shape. They contract and push against your weight. This applies an equal and opposite force (reaction) to the object (you, the jumper). Hooke's law determines the size of the force the spring exerts on the object. This reaction force sends you flying up.

BOUNCING MORE, JUMPING HIGHER

How high can you jump? On the trampoline, even beginners can make jumps of 16 feet! The height a person can reach on a trampoline depends on several factors—the number of springs, the stiffness of the springs, the elasticity of the trampoline fabric, and the height and weight of the jumper.

The laws of physics can help you bounce more and jump higher on a trampoline.

The greater the force pushing down on the trampoline surface, the greater the reaction force pushing back on the jumper. You can use your leg muscles to push down harder on the trampoline surface. This causes the trampoline and its springs to react with more force to push back against you and propel you higher.

As you reach higher peaks in the air, your body has more potential energy. As you fall back to the trampoline surface, the greater potential energy converts to more kinetic energy and greater force.

VOCAB LAB

Write down what you think each word means. What root words can you find to help you? What does the context of the word tell you?

compress, elastic collision, elastic limit, equilibrium position, inelastic collision, proportional, and **spring.**

Compare your definitions with those of your friends or classmates. Did you all come up with the same meanings? Turn to the text and glossary if you need help.

TEXT TO WORLD

Why do experts say only one person should be on a trampoline at a time?

The trampoline pushes back harder and launches you even higher on the next jump. Jumping in the center of the trampoline surface can also generate a more powerful push and a higher jump.

The trampoline system, including its fabric and springs, are built to be in balance. If you jump from the center, instead of from a corner or edge, all the springs can contribute equally and produce the greatest bounce.

Now that we've learned how physics can bounce you to new heights on a trampoline, let's move on to the next chapter, where we'll investigate how the lights and sounds of a band rely on physics to put on a great show!

DOUBLE BOUNCE

The double bounce is an interesting physics problem. This is not recommended, as it can lead to serious knee injury. But you can still learn the science! The double bounce is when two people jump together on the trampoline. Adding the extra person increases kinetic energy as the duo lands on the trampoline's surface. More elastic potential energy transfers to the trampoline's springs. Then, when the springs contract and push back, one of the two jumpers pulls their legs back in to delay their bounce. All the potential energy stored in the springs and the reaction force acts solely on the second jumper, who soars higher in the air.

KEY QUESTIONS

- **What makes springs a critical part of a trampoline?**
- **How do Newton's laws of motion affect what happens on a trampoline?**

STRETCH AND LAUNCH: ELASTIC POTENTIAL ENERGY

The springs of a trampoline store elastic potential energy. Elastic potential energy is a form of potential energy that is stored in elastic materials because of the way they stretch or compress. The amount of elastic potential energy stored in an object depends on the amount of stretch it has. The more the object stretches, the more elastic potential energy it stores. In this experiment, you'll test how the stretching of a rubber band impacts the amount of potential energy stored in it and the energy released when the band is released.

NOTE: This activity is best performed outside on a driveway or paved surface where there is a lot of space!

CAUTION: Always be careful when launching a rubber band that you don't hit any people or animals.

- **Draw a launch line on the ground with chalk.** This is where you will stand each time you launch a rubber band.

- **Hook a rubber band to the front edge of a ruler.** Pull it back 10 centimeters on the ruler and launch it! Have a friend mark with chalk where the rubber band lands. What happens to the potential energy when you stretch the rubber band? What happens to elastic potential energy when the rubber band is released?

- **Measure the distance between your launch line and the landing spot.** Record this data in your science journal.

- **Repeat the rubber band launch using the same 10-centimeter stretch multiple times, so you have multiple distance measurements.** Average the measurements to get a more accurate result.

- **Repeat the rubber band launch using several different stretch lengths.** Perform multiple launches at each length and calculate the average distance for each stretch length. Record all your data.

- **With your data, create a graph.** Plot the stretch length on the bottom of the graph and launch distance on the side of the graph. Mark a dot on the graph for the average launch distance for each stretch length. Is there a pattern to the graph's dots? Does it look like a straight line? Does it curve? Draw a line through the dots that best fits the data.

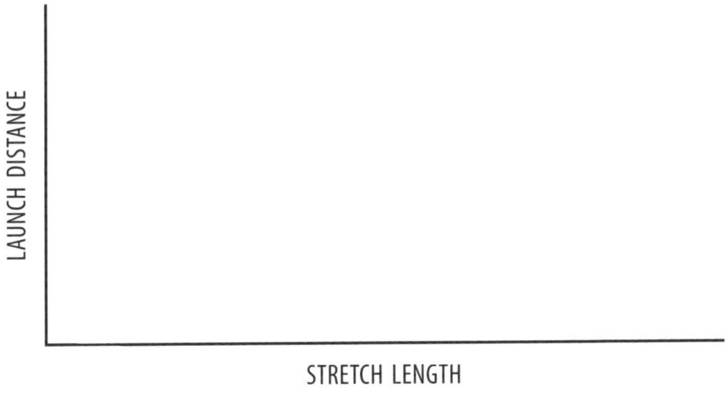

LAUNCH DISTANCE

STRETCH LENGTH

- **Based on your results, how does the stretch length affect launch distance?** How does this explain the relationship between elastic potential energy and kinetic energy?

To investigate more, repeat the experiment using rubber bands of different sizes and thicknesses. How does changing the rubber band affect your results?

BOUNCE HIGH ON A TRAMPOLINE

How does the weight of an object affect its bounce on a trampoline? In this experiment, you'll test several objects on a trampoline and observe how they bounce.

CAUTION: Always ask an adult before jumping on a trampoline.

- **Set up a yardstick or other measuring device on the side of the trampoline.** You want to be able to determine how high an object bounces in the air.

- **Position a digital video camera or smartphone to film the trampoline.** Make sure to include the yardstick in the picture frame.

- **From a fixed height, drop several objects, one at a time, on the center of the trampoline.** Record each drop. Vary the weight of the objects, including lighter objects and heavier ones.

- **Review the digital video frame by frame and note how high each object bounced.** Record your data in your science journal.

  - How did the object's weight affect bounce on the trampoline?

  - What physics principles are at work here?

- **Try varying the height from which you drop the items and repeat the procedure.**

  - How does the change in height affect your results?

  - How can physics help you explain what happened?

To investigate more, try bouncing one of your objects on different parts of the trampoline. What happens? Where does the object bounce the highest? Where does it bounce the least? Why?

Chapter 4

Form a Band: Waves of Sound and Light

EVEN INTANGIBLE THINGS OBEY THE LAWS OF PHYSICS!

What does the study of physics have to do with sound and light?

Sound and light travel in waves! Physics includes the study of how waves move through matter and how our brains receive the energy of those waves and turn it into sound and light.

·······················

As the audience cheers, the band takes the stage. The drummer beats a rhythm, the guitarist strums a medley of chords, and the pianist's fingers fly over the keyboard. As the music soars, a rainbow of laser lights flash, pulse, and swirl throughout the arena. It's a collection of light and sound for the eyes and ears. It's also an amazing demonstration of physics in action.

What do physics have to do with a musical concert? The sound you hear and light you see at a rock concert are made possible by waves. Waves are everywhere in the world. Some, such as ocean waves, you can see. Other types of waves, including sound waves and light waves, are invisible to the naked eye.

In physics, a wave is a pattern or motion, also called a disturbance, that **travels through space and matter.**

A wave transfers energy from one location to another, without transferring matter. Think of a breeze blowing through a field of wheat. It might look like the wheat is being carried along by the wind, but every plant is still rooted in the ground, not moving from its spot. What is moving through the field is energy.

Sound waves travel through the air and allow you to hear different sounds. Light waves move through space and allow you to see light and color.

Some waves, called mechanical waves, travel through a medium such as water, air, or the ground. Sound waves are an example of mechanical waves. Most of the time, sound waves travel through the medium of air. Without a medium for the sound wave to move through, you would not be able to hear sound.

Electromagnetic waves do not need a medium to travel through.

This type of wave forms when electric and magnetic forces act together. Because electromagnetic waves do not need air to travel through, they can move through space. Radio waves, microwaves, ultraviolet light, and visible light are examples of electromagnetic waves.

PROPERTIES OF WAVES

Remember the wheat field? Waves carry energy from one place to another. They do not carry matter. Even though it may look like a wave is carrying particles of matter, the particles do not travel with the wave. In the middle of the ocean, an ocean wave may appear to carry particles of water but the water is only moving up and down.

WALLACE SABINE AND ACOUSTICS

In the late 1890s, Wallace Clement Sabine (1868–1919), a physicist at Harvard University, was asked to improve the acoustics in one of the university's lecture halls located in the Fogg Art Museum. In a closed room, sound waves bounce off surfaces such as walls, ceiling, and furniture. Numerous reflections build up in the room and create reverberation. Sabine measured the hall's reverberation time, which is the amount of time it takes for a sound to fade away in a closed space. Then, he experimented with the sound-absorbing properties of materials and their effect on reverberation time. His work became the foundation for architectural acoustics, which uses science and engineering to create excellent sound within a building.

Scientists classify waves into two main categories: transverse waves and longitudinal waves. Transverse waves vibrate perpendicular to the direction the waves travel.

An ocean wave is an example of a transverse wave. It moves up and down, which is perpendicular to the wave's motion across the top of the water. A crowd performing "the wave" at a sporting event is also a transverse wave. People stand up and down as the wave moves around the stadium.

Their up-and-down motion is perpendicular to the wave's direction of travel.

Transverse wave

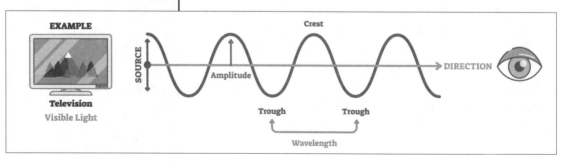

A longitudinal wave vibrates in the same direction as the wave. You can demonstrate a longitudinal wave with two people and a spring. Each person holds one end of the spring. When one person pulls their end of the spring back and forth (toward and away from the body), it creates a compression in the spring that travels down its length. Sound waves are another example of longitudinal waves. As sound waves move through a medium, such as air, the molecules collide with each other in the same direction the sound wave moves.

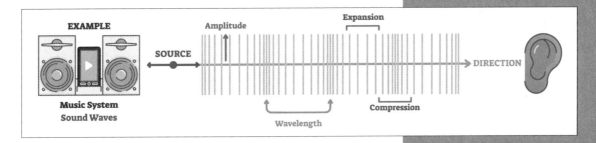

Longitudinal wave

Waves have certain properties that scientists use to describe them. Each wave has a high point called a crest and a low point called a trough. Amplitude measures the height of the wave. It also measures how much energy a wave has. Waves with higher amplitudes have more energy.

The wavelength is the distance between the highest point of one wave crest to the next crest. When a wave's crests are closer to each other, the wavelength is shorter. Waves with shorter wavelengths have more energy. When wave crests are farther apart, the wavelengths are longer and the waves have less energy.

Waves are also measured by their frequency, which is the number of waves per second. Frequency is the speed of the wave's vibration. The more waves per second, the higher the frequency of the wave.

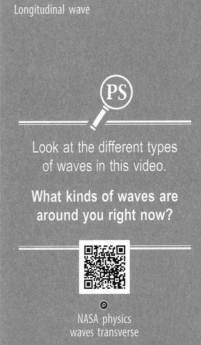

Look at the different types of waves in this video.

What kinds of waves are around you right now?

NASA physics
waves transverse

HOW SOUND WORKS

Look at this video to learn about longitudinal waves.

What longitudinal waves are around you right now?

NASA physics waves longitudinal

Have you ever been to a rock concert? What was it like? Did you feel like you experienced the concert with your whole body, not just your ears? That might have something to do with the vibrations.

Sound starts when something vibrates. The vibrating body causes the medium—usually air—around it to also vibrate. Have you ever put something small and light such as sand or rice on a speaker? The speaker's vibrations cause the object to bounce.

When a speaker vibrates, it creates waves that travel from the speaker through the air. Because air is made of matter, its particles carry sound well. It does not matter where you stand in the concert venue because the speaker's vibrations produce sound waves that travel in all directions.

You can hear the sound even if you are not directly in front of the speaker.

FLIP FACT

In a large stadium filled with noisy fans, it would be almost impossible to hear a band's instruments. Many musicians use electronic amplifiers to increase the intensity and loudness of sound waves. This allows the music to be more easily heard by the audience.

For a sound wave to travel, it must move through matter. Although most sound waves travel through air, they can also travel through other mediums such as solids and liquids. Some solids, including glass and metal, are good at carrying sound waves. Other solids, such as heavy fabrics and foams, do not carry sound waves that well. If you try to listen to a sound through a heavy fabric, the sound is muffled.

Sound waves also travel through liquid. Have you ever tried to talk to a friend underwater? It sounds a little different, but you can hear something. What about animals that live underwater? They use sound, too. Whales and dolphins communicate using complex patterns of clicks, whistles, and other noises. They also use echolocation, a method of sending and receiving sound waves underwater or through the air, to sense their surroundings.

Bats use echolocation to navigate through air in the dark.

Without matter to carry the sound wave, it will not travel. For example, if you tried to play music out in space, which is a vacuum, there is no matter to carry the sound waves. No music can be heard.

FLIP FACT

Because the human ear is more sensitive to high sounds, a high noise with the same intensity as a low noise may seem louder.

SOUND AS A LONGITUDINAL WAVE

When a sound wave travels through air, it causes air particles to vibrate and hit each other in a direction that is parallel to the direction of the wave's energy movement. This important characteristic makes a sound wave a longitudinal wave.

Imagine a slinky toy that is stretched horizontally. If you vibrate the first coils of the slinky horizontally, each individual coil begins to vibrate in a direction that is parallel to the direction of the overall energy of the wave.

Watch sound waves in action in this video.

How does the sound affect the sand?

SMUPhysics
Chladni Plate

As a sound wave moves through air, particles of air are displaced. In some areas, the air particles are compressed together—called high density— while in other areas, the air particles are spread out—called low density. This creates compressions and rarefactions in the air, or areas of high density and low density. They follow one another in an alternating pattern.

In a longitudinal wave, wavelength is measured as the distance from one compression to the next compression.

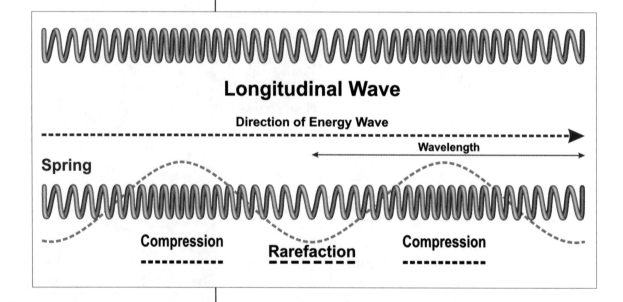

Longitudinal Wave

Direction of Energy Wave

Wavelength

Spring

Compression

Rarefaction

Compression

A wavelength always includes one compression and one rarefaction. In this way, sound waves are also pressure waves, with areas of high and low pressure that are created by the vibrations of the sound's source.

When you strum a guitar string, it vibrates back and forth. When the string moves in one direction, it pushes on the air particles and presses them together (compression). When it moves in the other direction, it leaves a space in the air particles and they spread out (rarefaction). The air particles that are pushed by the vibration of the string push on air particles next to them, and the pattern continues.

As the air particles push and bump each other, the sound wave travels outward from the guitar through the air. The air particles themselves do not travel. Instead, they vibrate back and forth in a direction parallel to the sound wave's motion.

As with any kind of wave, sound waves have frequencies and amplitudes.

A sound wave's frequency is measured by the number of vibrations per second. A high-frequency wave has many vibrations per second, while a low-frequency wave has fewer vibrations per second. Higher-frequency sound waves have a higher pitch, which means they produce a higher note.

Sound waves also have amplitude. Because a sound wave is a longitudinal wave, the vibrating particles of air move back and forth in the same direction as the wave. The wave's amplitude is the distance between the air particles where they are compressed. The closer the air particles are, the greater the wave's amplitude. Higher-amplitude sound waves produce louder sounds.

WAVE SUPERPOSITION

At a party, you can hear the noise of the crowd. You can also distinguish the voice of just one person. How is this possible when all these sound waves are traveling throughout the room? Wave superposition occurs when two or more waves travel through the same space in a medium together. Each wave maintains its own identity and is not affected by other waves in the same space. That is why you can hear your friend's voice amid all the noise and carry on a conversation.

....

FLIP FACT

All matter is made of atoms that are constantly in motion. When struck or strummed, all objects produce a natural frequency or frequencies.

HEARING SOUND

How do all these sound waves get inside your head so that you hear sound? How do you hear that band concert? Once again, it's all about vibrations!

Hearing is the process by which you pick up sound waves and attach meaning to them. Vibrations create invisible sound waves that travel through the air. Your ears enable you to detect and interpret these waves to hear sound.

The human ear consists of three parts: the outer ear, the middle ear, and the inner ear. Each part has a specific role in detecting and interpreting sound. The outer ear is made up of the fleshy outside part, the ear canal, and the eardrum. Sound waves enter through the fleshy outer ear and travel through the ear canal to the eardrum. When the sound waves hit the eardrum, it vibrates.

A portion of the eardrum is part of the middle ear. The middle ear contains tiny bones that vibrate when a sound wave hits the eardrum. These vibrations cause a reaction in the inner ear, which contains fluid and tiny, hair-like nerve cells. These nerve cells take the vibrations and transform them into electrical signals, which are sent to the brain.

The brain receives and interprets the electrical signals as sound. The brain makes meaning out of these signals so that you can understand and identify the sound. When any part of this process is disrupted, hearing loss can occur.

FLIP FACT

If a sound is too loud, its sound waves might cause so much vibration that they damage the eardrum, which can impair your sense of hearing.

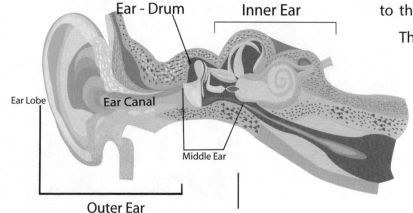

Ear - Drum

Inner Ear

Ear Lobe

Ear Canal

Middle Ear

Outer Ear

WHY ARE SOUNDS DIFFERENT?

Listen to the world around you right now. How many different sounds can you hear? Probably a lot! And they're all different. The sound of a dog barking is different from the sound of a violin. Some sounds are soft, while others are loud. The flute plays high notes, while the tuba booms low notes. You can even tell the difference between your friends simply by the sound of their voices. What makes one sound different from another sound?

Differences in sounds are caused by the characteristics of intensity, pitch, and tone. Amplitude is a measure of a sound wave's energy. The more energy the sound wave has, the higher its amplitude. As amplitude increases, intensity also increases. The intensity of a sound is the amount of energy a sound has over an area and can be measured in decibels.

Sounds with a higher intensity are commonly called louder. A soft whisper measures about 30 decibels, while drums measure between 90 and 130 decibels.

Pitch is another quality that makes sounds different. We use pitch to tell the difference between low and high sounds. Imagine playing two C notes on a piano, with the second C note one octave above the first. Although both sounds are the C note on the piano, you can tell the difference between them because their pitch is different.

Sounds that are too high frequency for humans to hear are called ultrasonic.

FLIP FACT

Listening to sounds greater than 85 decibels for a prolonged time may damage the human ear.

A sound's pitch depends on the frequency of a sound wave. Even though you played the same C note on the piano, the two sounds had different frequencies and you could hear the difference.

Scientists measure sound's frequency in hertz. One hertz equals one cycle of compression and rarefaction per second. A high-pitched sound has a high frequency, while a low-pitched sound has a low frequency.

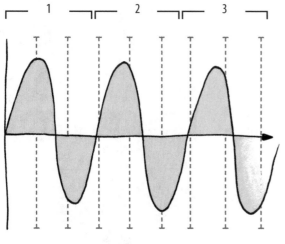

Wave A
(higher frequency, higher pitch)

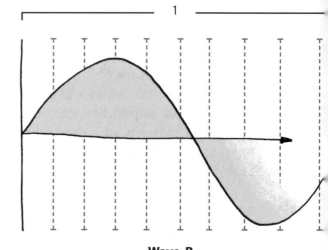

Wave B
(lower frequency, lower pitch)

The human ear can hear sounds with frequencies between 20 and 20,000 hertz.

Tone also helps distinguish sounds. A clarinet sounds different from a flute playing at the same pitch. And a new cello player sounds different from an experienced cellist, even when playing the exact same note.

Different tones explain this difference. When a sound source vibrates, it vibrates with multiple frequencies at the same time. These frequencies do not change the basic pitch of the sound but give the sound its own quality. Tone, sometimes called sound quality, gives a sound its specific identity.

CREATING MUSIC

Without sound, music would not exist. Every piece of music is made up of sound. We can hear music because of sound waves that travel through the air to our ears and brains. What makes music different from other sounds? Some sounds, such as a jackhammer, are unpleasant. Other sounds, such as the soft patter of rain against the roof, are pleasant. Yet neither sound is music.

Music generally has three properties that distinguish it from other sounds.

A musical sound has an identifiable pitch, a pleasing tone, and a repeating pattern or rhythm. Many different sound waves create music, all with different amplitudes and frequencies. When you learn to play music, you are learning how to control sound waves.

STANDING WAVES

When you pluck a guitar string or blow into a flute, you create vibrations, or mechanical waves, within the body of the instrument. These vibrations created within the instrument are a special type of wave called a standing wave.

Standing waves typically form when a wave bounces back and forth in a restricted area—such as a tube—which can be closed or open. For example, when you pluck a guitar string, the string's vibration is restricted by the fret bar at one end of the string and the guitar's bridge at the other end of the string. When you pluck the string, its wave bounces off each of these ends.

FLIP FACT

Dogs hear sounds at higher frequencies than humans. A dog can hear a high-frequency dog whistle while a human hears nothing.

As the wave moves back and forth between the string's two ends, standing waves are created.

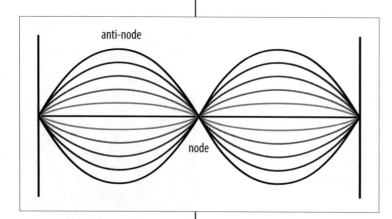
anti-node
node

A standing wave does not appear to be traveling from one end of the string to the other. Instead, it looks as though it is moving up and down while staying in place.

Even though the string is only restricted at its ends, some points in the middle of the string do not move at all. These points are called nodes. The points of the string that are in between two nodes and have the greatest motion from the center are called antinodes.

When an instrument is made in a specific shape, sound waves travel within it in a controlled, predictable way. The instrument creates consistent standing waves that make a certain tone. The consistent, specific tone separates the instrument's sound from other noise.

All musical instruments use standing waves to make music. People who make and play instruments know about standing waves and use their physics knowledge to create beautiful music!

HOW DIFFERENT INSTRUMENTS CREATE MUSIC

Do you play the drum, flute, or violin? Each type of instrument creates sound by causing matter to vibrate, which starts sound waves moving through the air. Remember, sound waves are longitudinal waves. The medium that the wave travels through vibrates in the same direction as the wave travels.

Most musical instruments can change the frequency of the sound waves they produce. This changes the pitch of the sounds and allows musicians to play high and low notes.

On a stringed instrument such as a guitar, the strings are about the same length and tension. So, why does each string sound different when you pluck it?

The sound waves produced by a string depend on the string's mass, tension, and length. If you look closely, you'll notice that the strings are different sizes. As a result, the mass of each string is different. The string with the smallest mass vibrates the most, so it has the highest frequency. As a string's mass increases, its frequency decreases.

ANTONIO STRADIVARI

Antonio Stradivari (1644–1737) is considered by many to be the most famous violin maker in the world. During his decades-long career, he and his sons made more than 1,000 stringed instruments. About 650 of those instruments survive today. While many of his instruments were violins, Stradivari also built violas, cellos, guitars, and even harps. All of his stringed instruments are known for their unmatched craftsmanship, materials, and sound quality. Each featured tiny, ornate details on the instrument body. In June 2011, a Stradivarius violin called the 1721 "Lady Blunt" Strad became the most expensive violin in the world when it sold for nearly $15.9 million at auction.

Music is an art of both science and emotion. Listen to this young guitar player.

How does he get such a variety of sounds from his instrument?

Marcino videos

To create a different note, the musician presses on the string until it contacts a fret. This shortens the string and increases the frequency of the wave it produces. The sound wave's pitch sounds higher. As a musician moves their fingers on the strings, they change the standing waves created and the notes the instrument produces.

To make music with a wind instrument such as a clarinet or flute, a musician blows air into or across the instrument's mouthpiece. This creates vibrations that start the column of air inside the instrument vibrating. The musician uses their fingers to open or close holes along the instrument body, which lengthens or shortens the length of the vibrating air column. This changes the wavelengths and therefore the frequency and pitch of the instrument's sounds.

On a percussion instrument such as a drum or xylophone, musicians strike the instrument with a mallet, drumstick, or even an open hand. Striking the instrument causes the drumhead or xylophone bar to vibrate. The vibrating drumhead or bar causes other parts of the instrument to vibrate as well, which amplifies the sound waves.

That is a lot of sound waves to keep organized!

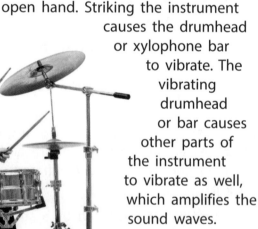

FUNDAMENTALS, OVERTONES, AND HARMONICS

As we've learned, musical instruments start vibrations that create sound waves within the body of the instrument. The longest wave that fits in the body is called the fundamental frequency. The fundamental is also the lowest pitch you hear. Yet the fundamental is only one of many pitches that the instrument produces. Parts of the guitar string are vibrating at frequencies higher than the fundamental.

Other frequency waves that exist in a musical instrument are called overtones. Frequencies that are whole multiples of the fundamental frequency are called harmonics.

Instruments come in different shapes and sizes and create vibrations in different ways. The different shape and size of each instrument produce different overtones. These overtones combine and form the instrument's recognizable sound.

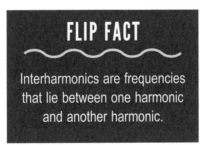

FLIP FACT

Interharmonics are frequencies that lie between one harmonic and another harmonic.

For example, a flute and a cello can play the same note with the same frequency. However, because each instrument produces different overtones, they sound different.

RESONANCE

Most musical instruments amplify sound waves with resonance. Resonance occurs when an object vibrates because of sound waves of a certain frequency. For example, when a drummer strikes the drumhead to make it vibrate, the entire drum and the air inside it also vibrate. This resonance amplifies the sound waves and makes the sound of the drum louder.

WAVE INTERFERENCE

When two or more sound waves are in the same space, they interact and affect each other. This is known as sound wave interference. Wave interference can be constructive or destructive.

In constructive interference, two waves line up and have the same frequency (pitch) and amplitude (volume). Their peaks and troughs line up with each other. The two waves are added together, which creates a wave that has twice the amplitude of the original waves. You hear a sound that is twice as loud as the original sound.

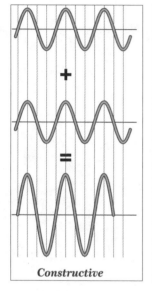

Constructive

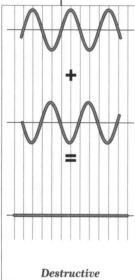

Destructive

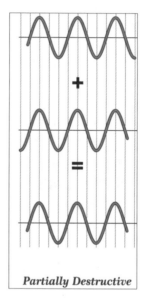

Partially Destructive

In destructive interference, two waves are not in sync. They come together with the peak of one lining up with the trough of the other, and vice versa. When added together, the sound waves create a diminished waveform. In some cases, they cancel each other out entirely and you hear nothing.

When two musical notes are played, the sound waves are simply added together to create a complex waveform. In music, we think of this combination as harmony.

Noise-canceling headphones use destructive interference.

As they detect sounds coming into the ear, they produce sounds with opposite peaks and troughs but the same amplitude, which cancels out the other sound wave and creates near silence.

When two sounds waves have similar but slightly different frequencies, or pitch, they combine to create a wave that has some points of constructive interference and some points of destructive interference. The volume varies at a regular rate and you can hear a pulse in the sound. To the ear, this creates a beat pattern.

Wave interference is an important part of music.

Musical sound waves interfere with each other just like other waves. When different musical notes are played together, they create complex wave patterns that produce pleasant sounds, called consonant, or unpleasant sounds, known as dissonant.

FLIP FACT

In an auditorium, designers often install padded walls or panels to absorb sound waves. The padding reduces echoing and sound wave interference, which improves the audience's listening experience. This helps improve the room's acoustics.

HEARING LOSS

When any part of the hearing process is disrupted, a person may experience hearing loss. For example, if the tiny bones in the middle ear do not pass along sound waves to the inner ear or if the eardrum doesn't vibrate when sound waves hit it, hearing loss can occur. Hearing loss can also happen when disease, injury, or another event disrupts the electrical signals being sent from the ear to the brain. Some causes of hearing loss are genetic and can be passed from parent to child.

HOW WE SING

Have you ever heard someone say that your voice is your instrument? When you sing, your body acts as an instrument to produce sound. First, you inhale a deep breath, and then, you exhale as you start to sing. The exhaled air moves through the windpipe and through the larynx, also called the voice box, which holds the vocal cords. The exhaled air makes the vocal cords begin to vibrate.

The vibration of the vocal cords is like the vibration of a stringed instrument. The vibrating cords produce sound. Inside the larynx, vocal cords are two small muscles that have a moist covering.

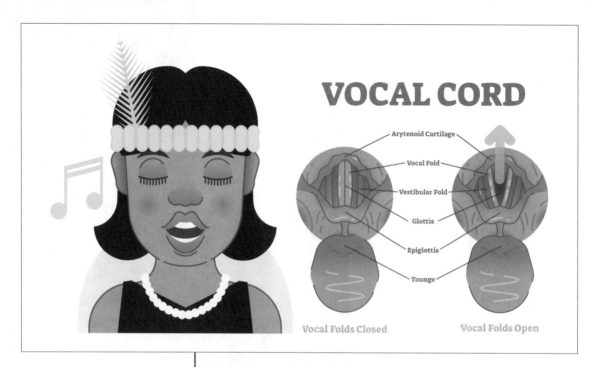

VOCAL CORD

Arytenoid Cartilage

Vocal Fold

Vestibular Fold

Glottis

Epiglottis

Tounge

Vocal Folds Closed

Vocal Folds Open

When you breath, the vocal cords are open, allowing air to move from your upper airway into your lungs. When you want to sing or speak, the vocal cords close. You exhale, which causes an increase in pressure that causes them to vibrate.

The vibrating vocal cords produce a buzzing-like sound. Although it's a sound, the buzzing tone doesn't sound much like the voice you know.

Resonance takes the buzzing tone created by the vocal cords and turns it into a beautiful voice or song by shaping and amplifying the sound waves created by the vocal cords. The length and shape of your vocal tract affect how the sound waves are shaped and their frequency. The higher the frequency, the higher the pitch. The body structures and cavities that the sound waves bounce off of also affect resonance. If you hum for a few seconds, you can feel resonance in the front of your face.

The most common type of hearing loss, which nearly everyone experiences as they age, is the breaking or damaging of the hair cells in the cochlea. This damage is often caused by loud noises, such as loud music. It's important to protect your ears from loud noises!

If you growl, you can feel resonance in the back of your throat. When the sound waves reach the mouth, you use your tongue, teeth, and lips to shape them into song and speech. Because each person is unique, no two voices are alike.

LIGHT AS A WAVE

Now that you know how a band makes music, let's take a look at the light show! At a music performance, light fills the stage. Spotlights shine on the performers. Laser lights pulse throughout the arena. What exactly is light? And how does it work?

Scientists describe light as a form of energy made of particles called photons. In physics, light behaves both as a wave and as a particle.

Light waves are a type of electromagnetic wave. All electromagnetic waves are made of two waves (one magnetic and one electric) that vibrate perpendicular to each other. Radio waves, microwaves, infrared rays, ultraviolet rays, gamma rays, and X-rays are other types of electromagnetic waves.

As with all waves, electromagnetic waves carry energy. But, unlike sound waves, electromagnetic waves can travel through a vacuum such as space and do not need a medium such as air, liquids, or solids.

All electromagnetic waves are classified by their wavelengths and frequencies, called the electromagnetic spectrum. The visible spectrum, which is light you can see with the naked eye, is only a tiny part of the different types of electromagnetic energy that exist.

FLIP FACT

How do you sing a high note or a low note? When you sing, the vocal cords vibrate at a certain speed or frequency, which affects the note's pitch. Higher notes have a higher frequency and lower notes have a lower frequency. The vocal cords can change frequency by changing the tension in the muscles in the vocal cords. Increasing the tension raises pitch, while decreasing tension lowers pitch.

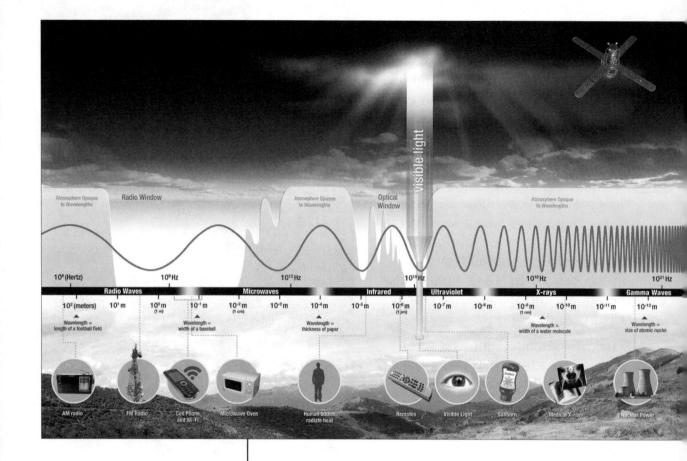

When a light wave hits an object, some of the light wave reflects or bounces off the object, while some of the light wave is absorbed by the object. How much light is reflected or absorbed depends on the object's surface.

The reflection of light waves is how we see color. Visible light contains all the colors in the color spectrum and each color has a different frequency.

Some colors have high-frequency waves, while others have low-frequency waves. When you see a red shoe, the low-frequency red waves are being reflected to your eyes, while the wavelengths of other colors are being absorbed by the shoe. When an object appears black, all the light waves are absorbed by the object and none reflects to your eyes.

When light waves move from one medium to another, such as, for example, when traveling from air to water, they refract or change directions. You can see refraction in action if you put a spoon in a glass of water. What happens? Do you see how the spoon appears to move to the side? This is an example of a light wave bending as it moves from air to water.

Light waves do not always travel in straight lines. When light waves pass near a barrier or obstacle, they bend around the obstacle and spread out. This is called diffraction.

To see an example of diffraction of light, hold your open hand in front of a light source. Slowly close two fingers while looking at the light transmitted between them. As your fingers get close to each other, you will see a series of dark lines parallel to them. The parallel lines are diffraction patterns created by the light bending around your fingers.

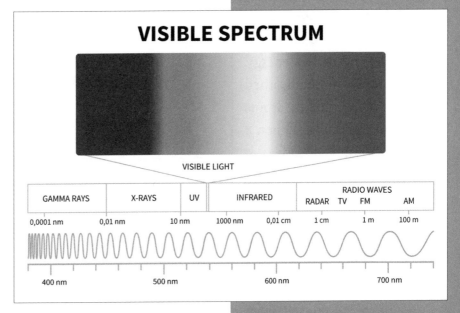

LASER SHOW SCIENCE

Now, back to the concert. To create an incredible laser light show, the show's designers rely on physics. As we've learned, light is made of waves. Visible light contains many waves that bounce all over the place. Each color of light has a different wavelength.

LIGHT AS A PARTICLE

Light also behaves like a particle and can interact with matter. A photon is a particle of light that has zero mass, no electric charge, is stable, and carries energy. Photons can be absorbed or emitted by atoms and molecules. When a photon is absorbed, it transfers its energy to the atom or molecule.

For example, when sunlight hits your body, your skin absorbs some of the light's photons. These photons transfer their energy to your skin and you feel warmth.

The human eye also interacts with photons. When photons strike your eye, the photon turns into electrical energy, which is transmitted to the brain to form an image.

We see this mixture of wavelengths as white light. Imagine the surface of a choppy lake during a storm. It's similar to the many individual waves moving in natural, visible light.

Laser light is an artificial light. Lasers produce a narrow beam of light in which all the light waves have similar wavelengths. They travel together with their peaks lined up, which is called being "in phase."

The result is a very intense and pure light that can be focused onto a tiny spot.

Unlike white light, which spreads out and gets weaker as it moves away from its source, laser light travels from its source in a straight line, which allows it to keep its strength across long distances.

A basic laser is made from a tube with mirrors at each end, one of which is partly transparent. Inside the tube is a material such as a gas, crystal, or liquid. To create a laser, a powerful light or other energy source adds energy to the material inside the tube and causes it to produce light.

For example, electricity might cause gas inside the tube to produce light. The light waves bounce back and forth off the mirrors inside the tube, which cause the material in the tube to produce more light waves. Some of the light waves escape through the partly transparent mirror and become a laser beam.

In a laser light show, the type of laser used determines the color and brightness of the laser light. Some shows use multiple lasers to produce multiple colors.

FLIP FACT

The word "laser" is an acronym for "Light Amplification by Stimulate Emission of Radiation."

A projector with tiny moving mirrors can move a single beam of laser light so fast that the human eye cannot see the individual beam. Instead, the audience sees fans, cones, and cascades of beams in the air. Specialized optics can split one beam into hundreds of individual shafts of light. Bounce mirrors reflect beams throughout an arena. Lasers can even be used to create graphics suspended in the air or projected on ceilings and walls.

Light shows are often combined with music, live performances, and other media, such as video. Using computers, the show's designers can time the laser light effects with the music or live performances.

See how much fun physics can be? In the next chapter, we'll pick up our joysticks and learn about how even video games run on—you guessed it—science!

VOCAB LAB

Write down what you think each word means. What root words can you find to help you? What does the context of the word tell you?

amplify, **diffraction**, **electromagnetic spectrum**, **frequency**, **medium**, **photon**, **refract**, **wave**, and **wavelength**.

Compare your definitions with those of your friends or classmates. Did you all come up with the same meanings? Turn to the text and glossary if you need help.

TEXT TO WORLD

Have you ever been to a rock concert? What was the experience like?

KEY QUESTIONS

- **How are sound and light similar? How are they different?**
- **Do you play an instrument? How can you use your knowledge of physics to improve your own playing?**
- **Why is the medium through which waves travel important?**

SEEING SOUND WAVES

Sound waves start at a source that vibrates. The vibrating source causes the medium—usually air—around it to also vibrate. These vibrating particles create waves that travel from the sound's source invisibly through the air. When sound waves reach your ear, your eardrum vibrates as part of the hearing process. In this experiment, you'll be able to "see" how sound travels and how these waves affect the eardrum.

- **Stretch some plastic wrap tightly across the open end of a pot or bowl.** The opening should be covered completely and be smooth.

- **Place about 1 tablespoon of dry rice on top of the plastic wrap.**

- **Hold a metal cookie sheet or baking pan near the bowl with the plastic wrap but make sure it does not touch the bowl.** What do you predict will happen when you make a loud noise? Why?

- **Test your prediction.** Using a metal spoon, bang the sheet or pan loudly.

  - What happens to the dry rice? How do you explain what you observed? Was your prediction right? Why or why not?

- **Vary the volume of the noise you are producing by changing how hard you bang on the sheet or pan.** What effect does this have on the rice?

  - How do you explain what you observe?

  - How does this experiment mimic how an eardrum reacts to a sound?

To investigate more, test other noises at different volumes and observe what happens to the rice each time. What do you observe? What conclusions can you make based on your observations?

SPLITTING LIGHT INTO COLORS

Light may look white, but it is made of up many colors. Scientists use a device called a spectroscope to study the colors in light. When light hits a reflective object, all the colors reflect and bounce off in different directions. The colors in light spread out and form a spectrum. In this activity, you'll build a simple spectroscope to view the spectrum of colors in light.

CAUTION: Never look directly at the sun through a spectroscope! You could damage your eyes. Instead, aim your spectroscope at the light as it bounces off a white wall.

Ideas for Supplies ▼

- cardboard tube
- black cardstock
- black duct tape
- old CD or DVD
- flashlight

- **Use scissors to cut a slit at a 45-degree angle near one end of the cardboard tube.** On the opposite side of the tube, directly across from the slit, cut a small rectangular viewing hole.

- **Use the tube to trace two circles on the black cardstock.** Cut out the circles. Tape one to the end of the tube near the slit and viewing hole. Make sure no light can enter.

- **Cut a straight slit through the center of the second cardstock circle.** Tape this circle securely to the other end of the tube. The slit should run in the same direction as the CD when inserted into the spectroscope.

- **With the shiny side facing upward, insert the CD into the 45-degree slit.**

- **Shine a flashlight into the top of the spectroscope.** Look through the viewing window. What do you see? Draw what you observe.

To investigate more, compare different light sources with the spectroscope. You can compare light from your cell phone, fluorescent light, LED, candlelight, and other light sources. What colors do you see? Is there any difference between different light sources? Artificial vs. natural?

Ideas for Supplies ▼

- shoebox
- variety of rubber bands of different lengths and widths but long enough to fit over a shoebox
- paper towel roll
- tape

To investigate more, check out an online virtual oscilloscope to "see" the sound waves produced by your guitar. An oscilloscope gives a visual picture of a live sound's waveform.

ⓟ
virtual oscilloscope

EXPLORE SOUND WITH A HOMEMADE GUITAR

A guitar uses strings to make sound and music. In this activity, you'll make a homemade guitar from common household materials and explore how this instrument produces sound.

- **Take a shoebox or other rectangular container and cut an opening in the top, or take the lid off completely.**

- **Stretch at least four different rubber bands over the box.** Try to pick ones that have different lengths or widths. Space them evenly across the open space of the box.

- **Tape one end of a paper towel roll to one of the shorter sides of the rectangular box.** It should stick out from the box like a guitar neck.

- **Experiment making sound with the guitar.** Strum and pluck the different bands on the guitar.

  - Which one makes the lowest sound?

  - Which makes the highest sound?

  - Can you explain why the different rubber bands make different sounds?

- **Try to re-order the bands on the guitar so they play notes from lowest to highest.** What type of rubber bands work the best?

Chapter 5 ▶

Video Game Sparks: Electricity

EVEN VIDEO GAMES NEED PHYSICS TO WORK, AND NOT JUST FOR YOUR CHARACTER!

PEW ZAP POW

Why do we need physics to play video games?

ELECTRICITY TRAVELS THROUGH THE WIRE ON YOUR CONTROLLER . . .

. . . INTO YOUR GAME CONSOLE, THEN OUT MORE WIRES . . .

. . . RIGHT INTO YOUR TV—ALL BECAUSE OF THE POWER OF PHYSICS!

Video games—and all electronics—are made possible by the flow of electrons through a circuit. From a simple circuit that lights up a light bulb to an extremely complex circuit that powers your gaming device, physics explains how they work!

Video games are everywhere! Gamers play on computers, special gaming consoles, smartphones, tablets, and more. From toddlers playing preschool games to adults battling in strategy games, almost everyone has played a video game.

Push a button and the game comes to life. Push another button to control the action on the screen. Sound flows from the computer or console's speakers and provides music and game-related sound effects. None of this could happen without electricity, a type of energy that powers computers and gaming consoles.

In fact, electricity powers just about every piece of technology in your home. **And what's behind electricity? Physics!**

WHAT IS ELECTRICITY?

To understand electricity, we need to first take a step back and look at the atom. Atoms are the building blocks that make up all matter. Atoms can be densely packed together to form a solid object or more spread out in a liquid or a gas.

Atoms contain three basic parts: protons, neutrons, and electrons. Protons and neutrons exist inside the nucleus of the atom, which is its center. Protons are small particles with positive electrical charges (+). Neutrons, unlike protons, have no electrical charge. Their job is to help stabilize the atom.

Together, an atom's protons and neutrons make up most of its mass. Electrons are negatively charged particles (-) that exist outside the atom's nucleus. The opposite charges of the electron and proton attract each other and hold the atom together.

The flow of electrons is what creates electricity.

In some atoms, when a force is applied to an atom's electrons, the electrons can break loose and travel to another atom. When many atoms are close together and some of their electrons travel from one atom to another in the same direction, the result is an electric current.

Some materials are more likely to have electrons that move from one atom to the next. These materials are conductive. If you apply energy to them, including the energy stored in a battery, their electrons will start moving.

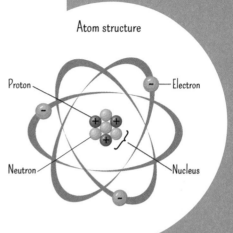

Atom structure

Proton — Electron — Neutron — Nucleus

Metals such as copper, aluminum, gold, platinum, and silver are examples of conductive materials. That's why the electrical wires in your electronics are made of metal—though they're also coated with rubber or plastic so you don't get a shock when you touch them.

FLIP FACT

Copper is the most used electrical conductor. It is used in wiring and electrical circuits worldwide.

CONDUCTORS VS. INSULATORS

Electric current flows more easily through conductors.
In a conductor, an atom's outer electrons are loosely bound to the atom. When an electric charge or voltage is applied, they move more easily from the original atom to the next atom. Typically, metals are the best conductors.

Materials that resist the flow of electric current are called insulators. They oppose the flow of electric current. Insulators protect us from electricity. They are often used to cover or provide a barrier between conductors to control electric current.

VOLTAGE GIVES A PUSH

What gives electrons an initial push to start moving? Voltage! Voltage comes from an energy source such as a battery and creates the force that pushes electrons through an electrical loop. Voltage is measured in units called volts (V). The higher the voltage, the greater the push it gives and the more electrons flow through the wire.

When electrons move from one atom to the next in the same direction, they form an electrical current.

Electric current is measured in units called amperes (A), or amps. When many electrons flow through a wire, the current is strong. Think about a river flowing downstream. When the river's current is strong, more water rushes down the river. Similarly, a higher voltage increases the electric current.

SLOWING DOWN WITH RESISTANCE

Voltage gives electrons a push to start an electric current. What happens when something gets in the way to slow or interrupt that current? Resistance! Have you ever kinked a garden hose when water is flowing through it? What happens? The water slows, right? That kink adds resistance to the flow of water through the hose.

Another way to think about resistance is to remember the way friction between a bicycle's brakes and the tires slows you down. In electric currents, resistance works the same way to slow the current. Resistance here is measured in ohms (Ω).

PUTTING IT ALL TOGETHER

Electrons, current, voltage, and resistance work together to produce electricity and power many devices in the world. Let's see how they come together to light an incandescent bulb.

Inside a light bulb, a metal wire called a filament is made of a conductive material. One end of the wire filament is connected to the metal side of the bulb's base, while the other end connects to the metal contact on the bulb's bottom.

When you connect a stored energy source such as a battery to the light bulb, it creates an electrical circuit. This closed path allows electric current to flow.

The battery provides voltage that pushes electrons through the circuit and creates electric current. The filament provides resistance to slow the flow of current in the circuit. As the electrons slow down to push through the filament's resistance, the filament itself heats up. It becomes so hot that it glows and generates light.

For the electrical circuit to work, it must be closed. If any point of the circuit is disconnected, the electric current stops flowing and the light bulb turns off.

Take a look at this article and videos to learn more about how electricity works!

Curious Kids how electricity work

UNDERSTANDING ELECTRICAL CIRCUITS

All electronics today, including computers and video game consoles, are based on electrical circuits. Harnessing electricity is the basis of electronics.

To better understand how basic circuits work, let's take a look at a water pipe system with a pump. The pump pushes water so that it flows throughout the entire pipe system. The pump is like a battery that provides power to an electrical circuit. Once the pump pushes the water, it continues to circulate through the pipe system unless something stops it.

A simple electrical circuit operates the same way. Every electrical circuit has at least three basic components: a conductive path, a source of electricity, and a load.

Electrons need a conductive path to travel along. This can be a wire made from conductive material or printed etches on a circuit board. The circuit must also have a source of electrical power, such as a battery, generator, or wall outlet. The source provides the voltage needed to get the electrons moving. A circuit must also have a load, which is an electrical component, such as a lamp or fan, that needs electrical power to operate.

OHM'S LAW

In an electrical circuit, what is the relationship between voltage, current, and resistance? How does a change in one affect the others? We can use Ohm's law to figure it out.

Ohm's law, named after Georg Ohm (1789–1854), who discovered it, is a basic law of electrical circuits. It states that current passing through a conductor is proportional to the voltage divided by resistance. The equation for Ohm's law is:

$$I = V \div R$$

current (amps) = voltage (volts) ÷ resistance (ohms)

Notice that in this equation, the symbol for amps is the letter I. The same equation can be re-written to calculate voltage ($V = I \times R$) or to calculate resistance ($R = V \div I$).

Ohm's law calculates how current flows through resistance when different voltage is applied.

We can think about this relationship using the water pipe example again. The amount of water flowing through the pipe represents current, the pipe's size represents resistance, while water pressure represents voltage. More water (current) flows through the pipe when more pressure (voltage) is applied. More water (current) also flows as the size of the pipe increases (lower resistance).

Understanding Ohm's law is the key to controlling current and voltage in a circuit. If you want a certain amount of current to flow through a circuit, you can calculate how much resistance or voltage you need. Ohm's law allows designers of video game consoles and all electronics to control the amount of current in the console's circuits so the device has just the right amount of power to run as designed.

SEMICONDUCTORS

Materials called semiconductors are essential to electronic circuits and digital devices. A semiconductor is partly like a conductor, which easily conducts electric current, and partly like an insulator, which resists electric current. Most semiconductors are made of silicon crystals mixed with other elements. Semiconductors are important in electronic devices because they allow electric current to flow in a single direction or only when certain conditions are met.

SERIES OR PARALLEL CIRCUITS

How current flows through components depends on how you design a circuit. In a series circuit, current runs through each component one by one in a pre-determined sequence. If one component fails, the flow of current through the entire circuit stops.

A series circuit is like a string of Christmas lights that goes dark when a single light burns out.

You can also design a circuit so that current runs through different components at the same time, in parallel. In a parallel circuit, part of the current runs through one component while another part runs through another component. If the Christmas lights are on a parallel circuit, when one light burns out, the other lights stay lit.

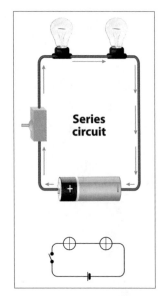

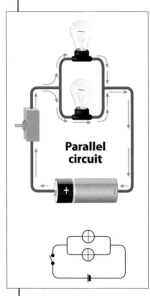

ADDING COMPONENTS TO A CIRCUIT

Although you can make a simple electrical circuit with only a battery, wire, and a light bulb, most electronics devices use a few more components to make them work. Common components include resistors, capacitors, diodes, transistors, and integrated circuits. Some electrical components control the flow of electricity, such as a dimmer switch that controls a light's brightness.

Other components powered by electricity perform a function, such as a speaker that produces sound. Some components detect a condition, such as light or heat, and then generate a current that produces a response, such as setting off an alarm. The type of components in a circuit and the way they are connected to each other determine what the circuit does. In one arrangement, components can create an electronic siren. Arranged another way, the circuit may control a flashing light.

A switch is one of the simplest components used to control the flow of electricity.

Switches are all around your house. You use a switch to turn lights, computers, ceiling lights, and other devices on and off.

Switches play an important role in electric circuits. Made of two pieces of metal that can connect or disconnect, switches control the flow of electric current.

When turned "on," a switch connects two wires to close an electrical circuit. Electricity flows through the circuit and the light, computer, fan, or other device powers on.

When turned "off," the switch disconnects two wires to open an electrical circuit. In an open circuit, electric current cannot flow. The devices connected to the switch—the light, computer, fan, or other device—power down.

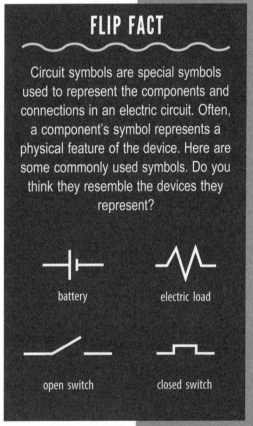

FLIP FACT

Circuit symbols are special symbols used to represent the components and connections in an electric circuit. Often, a component's symbol represents a physical feature of the device. Here are some commonly used symbols. Do you think they resemble the devices they represent?

battery

electric load

open switch

closed switch

Sensors are components that create a current when exposed to certain conditions. The generated current can then be used with other components to turn electronic devices on or off. For example, a motion detector includes a sensor. When the sensor detects the motion of a person walking up to your door, it generates an electrical signal. The signal flows through the device's circuit and turns on a light. Other types of sensors can detect light, sound, or temperature.

Electrical circuits can also power components to produce heat, light, sound, motion, and more.

In the example of the motion sensor, the circuit powers the light to turn on. Another type of circuit may supply electricity to a motor that causes it to rotate. Electrical circuits provide electricity to power speakers, lights, and more.

CONTROLLING CURRENT IN CIRCUITS

Within a circuit, some components have an important job. They control the flow of electrons through the circuit in a specific and precise way. Resistors slow down or "resist" the current as it passes through them.

The more resistance a circuit has, the less current flows through it. Resistors can therefore limit or control the current to specific components.

FLIP FACT

Some components, such as LEDs (light-emitting diodes), can burn out if too much current runs through them. By adding a resistor to the circuit, you can limit the amount of current that reaches the LED and prevent it from burning out.

Resistors can also reduce voltage to part of a circuit or control the current that goes into another component. For example, a resistor added to a transistor can help control how much the transistor amplifies a signal. Resistors reduce current by converting electrical energy into heat.

Capacitors are another common component found in electronic devices. Capacitors consist of two pieces of conductive material—metal—separated by an insulating material called a dielectric. Capacitors smooth out fluctuations in electrical current by attracting electrons with a positive voltage and storing them. This reduces the electrons flowing through the circuit and reduces the current. When the positive voltage is removed, the electrons leave the capacitor and the current increases.

In this way, a capacitor can add or remove electrons from a circuit to control current.

Transistors can switch small electric currents on and off. They can also transform small electric currents into larger ones to amplify a signal. In hearing aids, for example, transistors amplify the volume of sounds for those who have trouble hearing.

Millions of transistors are part of computer microprocessors. When transistors are connected, they can make logic gates, which perform basic decision-making tasks. Without transistors, home computers and laptops would not be possible.

DIODES

A diode is another component that can be used to control the flow of electrons. A diode is a simple semiconductor. It has two terminals and acts as a one-way valve for electrons. Electrons can pass through the diode in one direction but not the other direction.

Computer chips

Integrated circuits take many individual components and combine them on miniature circuit boards. Also called a chip, an integrated circuit is created on a single piece of semiconductor material. An integrated circuit can hold hundreds of resistors, capacitors, diodes, and transistors.

Because so many components can fit on a tiny board, integrated circuits can be complex, yet still incredibly small. You can also string together integrated circuits to build larger circuits to create almost any electronic device imaginable. For example, a video game console uses a complex network of integrated circuits that work together to produce sound and video and run the game.

ELECTRICITY POWERS ELECTRONICS

Electricity creates energy that flows around a circuit to power a variety of devices, including electric motors, heating elements, appliances, electric cars, lighting fixtures, and a wide range of electronics.

Who would have ever guessed that something as small as an electron could power so many things!

FLIP FACT

Wireless video game controllers use Bluetooth or infrared technology to send data to game consoles.

Computers, televisions, and gaming consoles use tiny electric currents that are carefully controlled and directed around a complex network of circuits to process signals and store and process information. The circuits inside these electronic devices are packed with components. Each has a special job and is linked to other components by wires or metal connections printed on a circuit board.

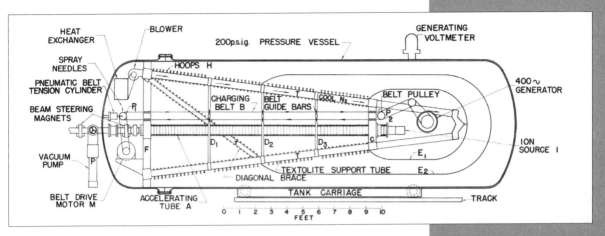

Take a look at a schematic for a Van de Graaff generator and tank drawn before 1949.

Credit: Berkeley Lab

Electronic circuits often use a printed circuit board to connect electronic components. The "wires" that connect the components are built into the board. Components can be soldered to the board's surface and connected to the circuit. In most cases, more complex electronic circuits can perform more intricate operations.

Often, drawings called schematics show how electronic circuits function. A schematic displays how the different components are connected. Schematic drawings use special symbols to represent the different components. By using the same symbols, different engineers can "speak" the same language on a project.

TALKING IN 1s AND 0s

Digital electronics store all types of information, from text and images to sound and video. This information is stored, processed, and communicated in a binary numerical code that uses only two digits:

1 and 0

HOW MUCH SPACE?

How many games can you download onto your gaming console? That depends on how big the games are and how much storage space the console has. Video games are measured in units called bytes. A megabyte (MB) consists of 1,000,000 bytes. A gigabyte (GB) consists of 1,000 MB or 1,000,000,000 bytes.

KEY QUESTIONS

- How many electrical devices are in your home? What would life be like without those?

- Why are switches so useful? What might gaming be like if there was no such thing as a switch?

- Why is it important for engineers to be able to communicate the details of an electrical device to other engineers?

TEXT TO WORLD

Do you play video games? What is going on in your gaming device when you are hitting buttons on your controller?

Why use binary digits? Inside a digital circuit, the binary digits exist as either electric currents (on or off) or as electric charges (present or absent). Numbers can be represented by a string of binary digits, called bits. Circuits produce electrical signals that represent bits. A group of eight bits is called a byte. A byte is a basic unit of information stored by computers.

How do common electronics use binary digits to represent information? When you touch a smartphone's screen, two binary numbers represent the specific coordinates of where you touched the screen. When you take a picture with a digital camera, the camera's sensors detect the brightness of each pixel in the image and binary digits represent the brightness of each pixel.

The next time you fire up the video games or browse the latest computer accessories on the internet, remember that physics makes it all possible! All electronics use the flow of electrons through circuits to power on, perform tasks, create sound, play video, and more. From the simplest circuit to the most complex video game, physics explains how it all works.

Almost everything you do—from running and jumping to singing and playing video games—relies on physics. Physics affects your skateboard tricks, how fast you snowboard, how high you bounce on a trampoline, the sounds you make when singing, and how your video games operate. You might say that physics is a part of every aspect of our lives.

Now that you've learned about the impact physics has on everything you do, go out and see how you can have some fun with physics!

BUILD AN ELECTRICAL CIRCUIT

All electronics today, including computers and gaming consoles, are based on electrical circuits. A simple circuit contains at least three basic components: a path for electrons to travel, a power source, and a load, or something that needs electricity to operate. In this activity, you'll build a simple circuit and see how it works.

Ideas for Supplies ▼

- 1 to 2 feet insulated copper wire
- scissors or wire cutters
- D battery
- small flashlight bulb with socket
- switch
- electrical tape

- **Cut the copper wire into three pieces.** Carefully remove about a quarter of an inch of insulation from both ends of each piece.

- **Use tape to attach the exposed part of one wire to the positive side of the battery.** Attach the other end of this wire to the left side of the light bulb.

- **Tape one end of the second wire to the negative side of the battery.** Attach the other end of the wire to one side of the switch.

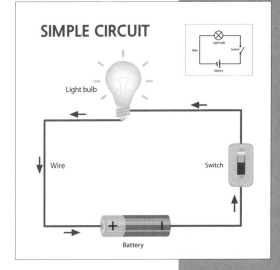

SIMPLE CIRCUIT

- **With the final piece of wire, attach one end to the other side of the switch.** Attach the other end to the right side of the bulb.

- **Figure out how to open and close the circuit.** How do you do this? Why does the bulb turn on and off? What happens if you disconnect one of the wires in the circuit? Will the light turn on? Why or why not? What happens to the flow of electricity if part of the circuit is missing?

To investigate more, what happens if you add a second battery to the circuit?

VOCAB LAB 📖

Write down what you
think each word means.
What root words can
you find to help you?
What does the context
of the word tell you?

**circuit, conductor,
current, electron,
insulator, integrated
circuit, resistance,
transistor,** and **voltage.**

Compare your
definitions with those
of your friends or
classmates. Did you
all come up with the
same meanings? Turn
to the text and glossary
if you need help.

To investigate more, use
the internet to research
more circuit symbols
and create a schematic
for a new design of
a circuit. What does
your circuit do? Did
you add any additional
components to your
circuit? What power
source did you use?

DRAW A SCHEMATIC
OF A CIRCUIT

Engineers use drawings called schematics to show
how different components are connected in a circuit.
Schematic drawings use special symbols to represent
components. Some of these symbols are:

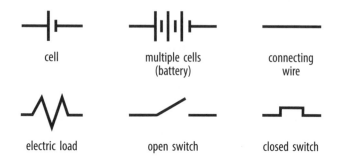

| cell | multiple cells (battery) | connecting wire |
| electric load | open switch | closed switch |

- **Use what you've learned above about circuit symbols.** Identify each component of the following circuit schematic.

- **Draw a schematic of the circuit you built in the "Build an Electrical Circuit" project.** Make sure to label each of the components. Why do engineers create schematic diagrams of circuits?

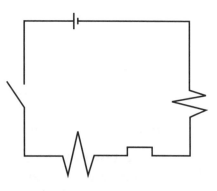

- **Give your schematic to a friend and see if they can use it to build your circuit.** How effective was your drawing? Do you need to make any changes?

SERIES VS. PARALLEL CIRCUITS

All circuits carry electric current when they are closed. Yet circuits can be set up in different ways. In a series circuit, all components are positioned one after the other so that electric current flows through each in order. In a parallel circuit, electric current is divided into two or more paths before joining back together to complete the circuit. In this activity, you'll design and build both types of circuits.

- **Using the supplies that you have on hand, come up with a design for a series circuit.** Include at least two bulbs in your design. Draw a circuit schematic for your design.

- **Build the series circuit.** For each piece of copper wire, carefully remove about a quarter of an inch of insulation from both ends of each piece. Connect the components using the wire and tape in the order pictured in your schematic.

- **Once completed, test the series circuit to make sure that it works.** Does the circuit operate as expected? What happens to the bulbs if you disconnect one part of the circuit?

- **Repeat the above steps to design, draw, and build a parallel circuit.** Include at least two bulbs in your design.

- **Once completed, test the parallel circuit.** Does the circuit operate as expected? What happens to the bulbs if you disconnect one part of the circuit?

- **What are the benefits of using a series circuit?** What are the disadvantages? What are the benefits of using a parallel circuit? What are the disadvantages? Which type of circuit powered a brighter light bulb? Why does this occur?

Ideas for Supplies ▼

- paper
- pencil
- several pieces of insulated copper wire
- scissors or wire cutters
- several D batteries
- several small flashlight bulbs with sockets
- 2 switches
- electrical tape

> To investigate more, try adding another load to your circuit designs, such as a small fan or buzzer. How can you add this component to each type of circuit?

GLOSSARY

absorb: to soak up a liquid or take in energy, heat, light, or sound.

acceleration: the rate of change in the velocity of an object.

acoustics: the way sound carries within a space.

aerodynamic: having a shape that reduces air resistance.

air resistance: the frictional force that acts on an object as it travels through the air.

alloy: a substance made of two or more metals or of a metal and a nonmetal, usually melted together.

ampere: a unit of measure for electrical current.

amplify: to make a sound louder.

amplitude: the peak of a sound wave, which is associated with volume.

angular momentum: the momentum of a rotating object.

antinode: the part of a standing wave that moves farthest from the center point.

applied force: a force that is applied to an object by a person or another object.

astronomy: the study of the stars, planets, and space. An astronomer studies astronomy.

atom: the smallest particle of an element.

axis: an imaginary line around which an object rotates.

balanced force: two forces of equal size acting in opposite directions.

BCE: put after a date, BCE stands for Before Common Era and counts down to zero. CE stands for Common Era and counts up from zero. This book was printed in 2021 CE.

binary: a base-2 number system (digits 0 and 1) used by computers to store data.

biology: the science of life and living things.

bit: the basic unit of information storage in a computer, consisting of a zero or a one.

byte: a group of eight bits that is treated as a single piece of information.

capacitor: an electrical component, such as a battery, that stores an electrical charge and releases it when needed.

center of gravity: the point on an object where all the weight is positioned.

chemistry: the study of the properties of substances and how they react with one another.

chord: a group of notes played together.

circa (c.): around that year.

circuit: when closed in a loop, a path that lets electricity flow.

circuit board: a board with connected electronic components.

closed system: a system that is not acted on by outside forces.

collide: to come together with solid or direct impact.

compress: to press or squeeze something so that it fits into a smaller space.

compression: a pushing force that squeezes or presses material inward. The part of a sound wave where air particles are pushed together.

concentrate: to bring or direct toward the center.

conductive: allowing electrical current to flow easily.

conductor: a material through which electricity moves easily.

conservation of energy: a principle in physics that energy cannot be created or destroyed, just transferred between objects.

conservation of momentum: a principle in physics that momentum cannot be created or lost in a system.

conserve: to maintain a total quantity, such as energy or mass, at a constant.

consonant: musical notes that sound good together when played at the same time.

constructive interference: the alignment of two sound waves with the same frequency and amplitude, which results in a wave bigger than the original wave.

crest: the highest point in a wave.

current: the flow of electrons in a circuit.

data: information in the form of facts and numbers.

decibel: a unit for measuring the volume and intensity of sound.

destructive interference: two sound waves that are not aligned so they cancel each other out.

dielectric: an insulating material.

diffraction: the bending or spreading of waves around the edge of an object.

diode: an electronic component that limits the flow of current to one direction.

direct relationship: a relationship between two variables such that when one increases or decreases, the other also increases or decreases.

displacement: the movement of an object from its original position.

dissonant: musical notes that do not sound good together when played at the same time.

ear canal: the pathway running from the outer ear to the middle ear.

eardrum: a thin membrane that separates the ear canal from the middle ear.

echolocation: the ability to find an object by sending out sound waves and listening for them to bounce back.

elastic collision: a collision in which the kinetic energy in the system is the same before and after the collision.

elastic limit: the farthest an elastic object can be stretched or compressed and still return to its original form.

elastic potential energy: potential energy that is stored in springs and other elastic materials.

electricity: energy created by the movement of electrons between atoms.

electromagnetic: one of the fundamental forces of the universe that is responsible for magnetic attraction and electrical charges.

electromagnetic spectrum: the entire range of electromagnetic waves.

electromagnetic wave: a wave, such as a light wave, that forms when electric and magnetic forces act together and that does not require a medium to travel through.

electron: in an atom, a particle with a negative charge.

emit: to send or give out something, such as smoke, gas, heat, or light.

energy: the ability to do work or cause change.

engineer: a person who uses science, math, and creativity to design and build things.

equilibrium: the state of balance between opposing forces.

equilibrium position: the natural position of a spring when it is not stretched or compressed.

etch: to make a pattern or design on a hard material by scratching or burning into the material's surface.

filament: the wire used as the conducting material inside a light bulb.

fluid friction: the friction resulting from an object moving through a fluid, such as a liquid or a gas.

force: a push or pull on an object.

freestyle: any snowboarding that involves performing tricks.

frequency: the number of times the crest of a wave passes a certain point in an amount of time.

fret: the space between two fret bars on a stringed instrument.

fret bar: a bar or ridge usually made of metal across the neck of a stringed instrument.

friction: the resistance that one surface or object encounters when moving over another.

fundamental science: a branch of science that is central to many other branches of science.

gravitational potential energy: the energy stored in an object as the result of its height above Earth.

gravity: the force of attraction between two objects with mass.

half-pipe: in snowboarding, a U-shaped ramp or runway.

harmonic: a frequency that is a multiple of the fundamental.

harmony: a set of musical notes played at the same time that are part of a chord.

heliocentric: the belief that the sun is the center of the solar system.

hertz: a unit for measuring the frequency of a sound.

horizontal: straight across from side to side.

incline: a slope.

inclined plane: a sloped surface that connects a lower level to a higher level.

inelastic collision: a collision in which kinetic energy is not conserved.

inertia: the tendency of an object to stay at rest or stay in motion unless acted on by a force.

infrared: an invisible type of light with a longer wavelength than visible light, which can also be felt as heat.

insulator: a material that resists the flow of electrical current.

intangible: something that is not physical.

integrated circuit: a tiny circuit board with many electronic components and their connections.

intensity: the amount of energy a sound has across an area.

interact: how things act when they are together.

inverse relationship: a relationship between two variables such that when one increases, the other decreases, and vice versa.

joule: a unit of energy.

kinetic energy: the energy of an object in motion.

larynx: the part of the throat that holds the vocal cords.

laser: a concentrated source of light made of one wavelength, or color.

linear: in a straight line.

load: the object that uses the electricity in a circuit.

GLOSSARY

logic gate: an electronic circuit that takes one or more inputs, analyzes them, and produces one output.

longitudinal wave: a wave that vibrates in parallel to the direction that the wave is traveling.

magnitude: size.

mass: the amount of material that an object contains.

matter: any substance that has mass and takes up space.

mechanical wave: a wave, such as a sound wave, that travels through a medium such as water, air, or the ground.

medium: a substance or material that carries a wave in physics.

meteorology: the study of weather and climate.

microscopic: something so small that it can be seen only with a microscope.

molecule: a group of atoms bound together to form matter.

momentum: the product of the mass and velocity of an object.

motion: a change in position during a unit of time.

net force: the sum of the forces acting on an object.

neutron: in the nucleus of an atom, a particle that has no charge.

Newton (N): the unit used to measure force.

Newton's first law of motion: an object at rest remains at rest and an object in motion stays in motion unless acted upon by an outside force.

Newton's second law of motion: acceleration is directly proportional to the force on an object and inversely proportional to the mass of that object.

Newton's third law of motion: for every action, there is an equal but opposite reaction.

node: a point in a standing wave that does not move from the center point.

nucleus: the center of an atom.

octave: the eight-step interval between two notes in a scale.

ohm: a unit of measure for the resistance to an electrical current.

Ohm's law: electrical current passing through a conductor is directly proportional to voltage and inversely proportional to resistance.

optics: the study of the properties and behavior of light.

orbit: the elliptical or curved path a body takes around an object.

overtone: a frequency produced on a musical instrument in addition to the fundamental tone.

parallel circuit: an electrical circuit with several different paths.

particle: a tiny piece of matter.

perpendicular: when an object forms a right angle with another object.

phenomenon: an observed event. Plural is phenomena.

photon: a particle of light.

physics: the study of matter, energy, and motion, and how they interact with each other. A physicist studies physics.

pitch: the highness or lowness of a sound.

pivot point: a point around which an object spins or rotates.

pixels: the small dots that make up a digital image.

potential energy: stored energy.

pressure waves: waves that create variations of pressure in whatever material they are passing through.

propel: to push or move something in one direction.

properties: characteristics, qualities, or distinctive features of something.

proportional: corresponding in size or amount to something else.

proton: a positively charged particle within the nucleus of an atom.

pumping: a technique that snowboarders use to increase their speed.

quantum physics: an area of physics that studies the microscopic world and its particles.

radiation: energy in the form of waves or particles.

radius: the distance from the center of a circle or sphere to its edge or circumference.

rarefaction: a low-density area of a longitudinal wave.

reaction: resistance or opposition to a force, influence, or movement.

reference point: in motion, something that lets you compare what is moving and what is not.

reflect: to redirect something that hits a surface, such as heat, light, or sound.

refract: to change direction.

relative: compared to something else.

resistance: a force that slows down another force. The slowing of a flow of charge through an electric circuit.

resistor: an electronic component that limits the amount of electricity flowing through it.

resonance: the vibration of an object because of sound waves of a certain frequency.

rhythm: a regular beat in music.

rolling friction: the friction that acts on an object as it rolls over a surface.

rotational motion: movement around the center of something.

scalar quantity: a physical quantity that has only magnitude.

schematic: a drawing of an electrical circuit.

semiconductor: a material used in electronics that has both conductive and insulating properties.

sensor: an electronic device that detects or measures a physical property such as light, sound, or heat and responds to it.

series circuit: an electrical circuit with only one path.

silicon: a nonmetallic element found in clay and sand, often used to make semiconductors.

sliding friction: the friction resulting from one object sliding across another object.

solder: to fuse metal together.

spectrum: a range of things with similar qualities.

speed: the distance an object travels in a unit of time.

spring: a coil of metal that stretches when a force is applied and returns to its original form when the force is removed.

spring constant: the stiffness of a spring.

standing wave: a combination of two waves moving in opposite directions with the same amplitude and frequency.

static friction: the friction between two objects that are not in motion relative to each other.

stationary: not moving.

subatomic: relating to the particles that make atoms, such as neutrons, protons, and electrons.

substance: matter, the material that something is made of.

supernatural: something attributed to an unseen force beyond the laws of nature.

superposition: the action of placing one thing on or above another.

sustainable: a process or resource that can be used without being completely used up or destroyed.

switch: a device that controls the flow of electricity through a circuit.

system: an organized collection of parts that work together to achieve a goal.

technology: the tools, methods, and systems used to solve a problem or do work.

telecommunications: technology concerned with communication across a distance.

tension: a pulling force that pulls or stretches an object.

terminal velocity: the greatest velocity a falling object reaches.

thermal energy: heat energy.

tone: the quality of a sound.

torque: the amount of force it takes to make an object turn or spin.

transistor: a component that can serve as an on/off switch in electronic circuits, as well as amplify electronic signals.

translational kinetic energy: the energy created by motion from one location to another.

transverse wave: a wave that vibrates perpendicular to the direction in which the wave is moving.

trough: the low point in a wave.

ultrasonic: involving sound waves with a frequency above the upper limit of human hearing.

ultraviolet (UV): a type of light with a shorter wavelength than visible light, also called black light.

unbalanced force: forces of unequal size acting in opposite directions.

universal gravitation: Isaac Newton's theory that every mass in the universe attracts every other mass.

vacuum: a space that is empty of matter.

vector: the magnitude and direction of a force, often represented by an arrow.

vector quantity: a physical quantity that has both magnitude and direction.

velocity: the speed of an object in a particular direction.

vibrate: to move back and forth quickly.

visible light: wavelengths that the human eye can see.

voltage: the force that moves electrons in an electric current.

wave: a curving movement in water, air, ground, or other object.

wave superposition: two waves traveling through the same space but not affected by one another.

wavelength: the distance from the crest of one wave to the crest of the next wave.

weight: a measure of the force of gravity on an object.

X-ray: a high-energy wave emitted by hot gases in the universe.

RESOURCES

BOOKS

Challoner, Jack. *STEM Lab*. DK Children, 2019.

Hile, Lori. *The Science of Snowboarding*. Capstone Press, 2014.

Macaulay, David. *The Way Things Work Now*. HMH Books for Young Readers, 2016.

McKinney, Donna B. *STEM in Snowboarding*. Abdo, 2017.

Schwartz, Heather E. *Snowboarding*. Lucent Books, 2011.

Smibert, Angie. *Fairground Physics: Motion, Momentum, and Magnets with Hands-On Science Activities*. Nomad Press, 2020.

Sohn, Emily. *Skateboarding: How It Works*. Capstone Press, 2010.

Wood, Matthew Brenden. *Projectile Science: The Physics Behind Kicking a Field Goal and Launching a Rocket with Science Activities for Kids*. Nomad Press, 2018.

WEBSITES

American Museum of Natural History – Physics: amnh.org/explore/ology/physics

Crash Course Physics (PBS Digital Studios/Crash Course): youtube.com/watch?v=OoO5d5P0Jn4&list=PL8dPuuaLjXtN0ge7yDk_UA0ldZJdhwkoV

The Physics Classroom: physicsclassroom.com

Physics for Kids Ducksters: ducksters.com/science/physics

Physics for Kids Science Kids: sciencekids.co.nz/physics.html

Physics for Kids – Real World Physics Problems: real-world-physics-problems.com/physics-for-kids.html

Radar's Physics 4 Kids: physics4kids.com

The Great Courses Plus: thegreatcoursesplus.com/physics-in-your-life

RESOURCES

SELECTED BIBLIOGRAPHY

DK. *The Physics Book: Big Ideas Simply Explained*. DK, 2020.

Holzner, Steven. *Physics I for Dummies*. John Wiley & Sons, 2011.

Holzner, Steven. *Physics II for Dummies*. John Wiley & Sons, 2010.

Kuhn, Karl F., and Frank Noschese. *Basic Physics: A Self-Teaching Guide*. John Wiley & Sons, 2020.

Skibba, Ramin. "Olympic Big Air Snowboarders Use Physics to Their Advantage." *Scientific American*, February 2, 2018.

Stone, Kate, and Jonathan Trinastic. "Science of Skateboarding: Half-Pipe Physics." *Science Connected Magazine*, June 8, 2017.

Wolfson, Richard. *Physics in Your Life*. The Teaching Company, 2004.

QR CODE GLOSSARY

Page 12: cudl.lib.cam.ac.uk/collections/newton/1

Page 18: youtube.com/watch?v=kkviQ41u0eQ

Page 21: nasa.gov/stemonstrations-newtons-third-law-rocket-races.html

Page 25: youtube.com/watch?v=sfbiO9dAGBQ

Page 26: youtube.com/watch?v=FBKqdjyrPQw

Page 30: instructables.com/Be-a-scientist:-make-your-own-force-meter

Page 39: youtu.be/3TY6ujT_3i4

Page 45: youtube.com/watch?v=he03dVkhLTM

Page 48: youtube.com/watch?v=_eMH07Tghs0

Page 49: fis-ski.com/en/snowboard/park-and-pipe/pipe-and-slope/news-multimedia/news/2020-21-fis-snowboard-big-air-and-slopestyle-season-preview

Page 57: youtube.com/watch?v=8rbxcHSfCe0

Page 61: youtube.com/watch?v=sgDcfcCRmio

Page 71: youtube.com/watch?v=njPwKoa3vIl

Page 72: youtube.com/watch?v=G-KGTambZtl

Page 73: youtube.com/watch?v=YedgubRZva8

Page 82: marcinofficial.com/video

Page 94: academo.org/demos/virtual-oscilloscope

Page 99: theconversation.com/curious-kids-how-does-electricity-work-118686

INDEX

INDEX